THE DREADFUL DECADE

U. S. Grant

THE DREADFUL DECADE

*Detailing Some Phases in the History of the United
States from Reconstruction to Resumption*

1869-1879

By DON C. SEITZ

ILLUSTRATED

GREENWOOD PRESS, PUBLISHERS
NEW YORK   1968

To
JOHN LANGDON HEATON

FOREWORD

In the decade between what was called "Reconstruction" and the resumption of specie payments, the United States underwent some strange experiences in the way of political, physical, moral, military and financial calamities. It is to chronicle the more unusual of these incidents that this book is written. It points no moral; it simply tells the tale.

D. C. S.

CONTENTS

CONTENTS—Continued

C O N T E N T S—Concluded

THE DREADFUL DECADE

CHAPTER I

RECONSTRUCTION

Aftermath of War—Problems South and North—The Ku Klux
Klan—The Colored Vote—Carpetbaggers and Their Rule of Ruin—
Military Government in Conquered States—Fifteenth Amendment.

To RECOVER readily from the consequences of a
great convulsion such as that which accompanied
the War between the States is a thing not readily
accomplished. This is especially true since it involved the complete disruption of the long-estab-
lished social and industrial order following the
extinction of slavery in the Southern States, the
introduction of new and ignorant elements into
politics, and above all, a struggle to retain power
on one hand and to regain it on the other. The adjustments of differences by the sword were not the
results of clean surgery. The wounds festered and
lingered, developing much "proud flesh," as the
surgeons say. A few "clasped hands across the
bloody chasm," but most did not. North and
South are still at variance and always will be. Sec-
tionalism is inevitable—a part of the principle of
competition that asserts itself everywhere between

races and localities. Without it, the world would become flat and tame.

Besides this, the war was fratricidal. Being a family affair, the South considered itself "licked," not conquered. It smarted, but did not yield obeisance or meekly lay its head under the heel.

The immediate reactions from the war had not been severe. President Johnson appointed civil governors in the various states and matters were mending in better fashion than could well have been expected, when the radical elements in Senate and House began their meddling. A tax of three per cent. was laid on cotton, later reduced to two and one-half, without rebate for export, which burdened the planters heavily. Something like five million bales had been found stored in the cotton territory. Confiscated by the government, it should have made a return of five hundred million dollars to the Treasury. Simeon Draper, who had been collector of the port of New York under President Lincoln, was made United States cotton agent to handle all of the confiscated fiber taken east of the Mississippi, and William T. Mellen, of Cincinnati, received a like award for that taken west of the big river. Draper received twenty-five per cent. for his services, and died a very rich man. There was more in the business than commissions.

The tax endured from 1866 to 1868, and during this time the planters of Alabama paid

$10,388,072.10 into the National Treasury; those of
Georgia, $11,897,094.98 and those of Louisiana,
$10,098,501. The other states gave up in propor-
tion. Southern senators and congressmen had been
turned back from Washington, and the states were
taxed without representation. The war cry that
bred the Revolution of 1776 was ignored by the
congressional majority. Thus it will be seen that
the South was doing business, but under highly
irritating, burdensome conditions. Jefferson Davis was in irons at Fortress Monroe and Thaddeus
Stevens was calling for blood, while Charles
Sumner, not content with having the slaves freed,
wished to give them power over their former owners. Between them, Stevens and Sumner contrived political vexations that checked prosperity,
kept wounds open and led to rough reprisals and
petty civil war.

Although Lincoln abolished slavery by proclamation, the country did not at once accept the
decision by legal enactment. The Thirteenth
Amendment, though carried in the Senate, received less than the necessary two-thirds vote in
the House, in 1864. The reelection of Lincoln
followed, and, taken as a mandate, brought the
amendment again before the same House. It
passed, February 1, 1865. The amendment
simply provided that "Neither slavery nor involun-
tary servitude, except as a punishment for
crime . . . shall exist within the United States,

[15]

or any place subject to their jurisdiction." There were ninety-four Republicans, sixty-four Democrats, and twenty-five "Union" border-state congressmen in the House. Eight of the Democrats did not vote; eleven said "aye," as did thirteen of the border-state men. The rest who supported the amendment were Republicans.

The states promptly confirmed the measure. As this failed to define the political status of the slaves, a fear smote the Republican leaders that the South would easily leap into the saddle when fully refreshed. Thaddeus Stevens, of Pennsylvania, therefore introduced on January 31, 1866, a fourteenth amendment, which laid down seemingly insuperable obstacles for the South. It provided, first, that "all persons born or naturalized in the United States . . . are citizens of the United States, and of the State wherein they reside," and that "no State shall make or enforce any law which shall abridge the privileges or immunities of citizens." It did not specifically give the ballot to the former slave, but provided that when "the right to vote" was abridged in any state, its representation in Congress should be cut down to fit the actual number of those permitted to vote—not a very drastic punishment, even if enforced, which it is not. It validated debts of the states and the Federal Government incurred in suppressing the civil conflict, and outlawed those of the Confederacy. It also rendered invalid any

[16]

claims for the loss of slaves by emancipation or flight, the latter point abolishing the legal status of property in Africans under the Fugitive Slave Act. It was passed June 13, 1866, by a vote of one hundred and twenty to thirty-two in the House—the latter all Democrats.

The southerners were required to accept these conditions before coming back into the Union. They were rejected by all except Tennessee, and so became the prelude to the period of congressional "Reconstruction" though it was in reality anything but reconstruction, if the word be properly defined.

January 3, 1867, Thaddeus Stevens, leader of the Republican radicals, brought up a bill he had previously fathered, calling for a system of rule in the South, declaring that anarchy had existed for two years and it was time to bring it to an end. His measure provided for dividing the section into five military districts, each to be presided over by an officer to be selected by U. S. Grant, Commander-in-Chief of the Army. These overseers were to preserve peace and maintain order, using legal tribunals or anything else convenient for the purpose. After fierce contention in House and Senate, it passed February 20, 1867, but was vetoed by President Andrew Johnson on March second. Both houses promptly repassed it over his veto, Johnson having few friends in either party. There was no enabling clause, so it was tinkered up by the new Congress and the amended measure passed finally on March twenty-third, covering Virginia, North Carolina, South Carolina, Georgia, Florida, Alabama, Mississippi, Louisiana, Arkansas and Texas in its operations. It now provided that the president should assign the military commanders to the five districts, none to be below the rank of brigadier-general. The War Department was required to provide a sufficient force to make each commander authoritative, and each was permitted to use local courts or courts-martial, as he pleased, in protecting life and property or preserving order. States could not interfere with these generals. They were permitted to hold elections for the purpose of adopting constitutions that would grant universal suffrage, and that would elect legislatures to adopt the Fourteenth Amendment, by which all citizens of "whatever race, color, or previous condition" might vote, unless outlawed by their part in the rebellion. Accepting the Fourteenth Amendment under these conditions, representatives to Congress and members of the Senate were to be admitted from the obedient state. Then the military government would let up. The generals were to register the voters and to see that only the right kind voted. These were to take an ironclad oath of allegiance to the Union. One of the most important places where the troops were to preserve order was at the polls! This ill-advised legislation at once became

RECONSTRUCTION

the excuse for the use by the South of an extraordinary organization which lives in history as the
Ku Klux Klan.

Pursuant to the law the War Department as-
signed Major-General John A. Schofield to the
First District, Virginia, with headquarters at
Richmond; Major-General Daniel E. Sickles to
the Second District, North and South Carolina;
Major-General George H. Thomas to the Third
District, Georgia, Florida and Alabama; Major-
General E. O. C. Ord to the Fourth District, Mississippi and Arkansas; Major-General Philip H.
Sheridan, Fifth District, Louisiana and Texas.
Sickles was a volunteer general and had lost his
leg at Gettysburg. He had been a Democratic
congressman from New York before the war. The
others were regulars. Each of the five districts
was well garrisoned.

The franchise remained a burning question, not
as to conferring deserved or desired rights upon
the negroes, but as a means of preserving the
power of the Republican party. There were
enough whites in the majority of the states of the
South to outvote the negroes, so that the section as
a whole was pretty certain to be controlled by a
party opposed to negro suffrage anyway. Republican power lay, therefore, in the North, and here
it was by no means certain. The Democrats
showed surprising strength. It therefore occurred
to Senator William M. Stewart, of Nevada, that

[19]

a specific statement of voting rights for the blacks would add those of the North permanently to the Republican strength, since their right to vote was not likely to be disputed outside the South. He accordingly devised a fifteenth amendment, reading: "The right of citizens of the United States to vote shall not be denied or abridged by the United States or by any State on account of race, color, or previous condition of servitude. The Congress shall have power to enforce this article by appropriate legislation."

In the debate, Oliver P. Morton, Senator from Indiana, pointed out plainly that this only operated against "race, color and previous condition of servitude," and that it would be easy to evade it by educational or property qualifications. This he prophesied would result when once the conservative Democrats regained control in the South, as it did. No southern state has lost in representation by reason of this practise of depriving negroes of the franchise, and no Congress has had the temerity to stop it.

Despite Morton's plea, the measure passed the Senate at three o'clock on the morning of February 26, 1869. The House had already carried it. Enough states accepted the amendment to put it in the Constitution. By making the negro eligible for office, and by protecting him with federal bayonets in his right to vote, it ushered in the most reprehensible phase of "reconstruction."

RECONSTRUCTION

The task of the various military commanders was more than disagreeable. They were compelled to rule over people of their own blood who hated and looked down upon them because of their calling, while at the same time they were forced to protect the blacks. Women are sentimentally supposed to suffer more from war than men, but the southern women were more difficult to manage. They spat on flags, ostentatiously walked in the mud rather than pass under a federal banner, and in their devotion to the lost cause made the social situation intolerable for the northern soldiers. Most of the southern men sensibly accepted the situation. Not so the suffering fair ones. Then, as a real grievance to the southerners, many colored troops were kept in the garrisons.

Another anomaly was a sudden fear of the negro, who, during the whole period of the war, with the South at his mercy, had not had recorded against him a single outrage affecting life, person or property, on the defenseless plantations, in shining contrast to the record of revolt in Hayti, where rebellious slaves butchered and ravished with incredible savagery!

This fear was not justified by any real events. So far as the records show, the black people behaved well, but expanded their chests under liberty and began to be "as good as anybody," in their minds and, as far as ignorance would permit, in their manners. The younger ones, who had not been well-broken under slavery, were assertive, but worse than this, the "submerged" white class became competitive in social assumption, while the more aristocratic element tended to keep in the background and allow the leaven of evil to work uncontrolled in both classes. The old slaveholders did not hate the negro; they regarded him as they would a horse or a dog. With the "poor whites," it was different. They had been starved by the monopoly of slave labor, not only on the farms, but as workmen in the towns. Colored blacksmiths, carpenters and painters among the slaves leased by their owners had shut white men out of trades that rightfully belonged to them. Politically and socially they had neither power nor position. The negro house-servants, who were in close touch with the "fine folks," looked down upon non-slaveholding whites. No wonder there was race hatred when the poor whites entered upon a struggle for equality with the enfranchised blacks. It did not come from a sense of superiority, but from an innate doubt that perhaps, after all, they were no better than the "niggers." They knew they had not been as good in the estimation of the well-to-do.

The loss of leadership growing out of the proscription of the men who had been foremost in the war, and the withdrawal of others of their type from any effort to manage public affairs, added to the difficulties. There was a well-defined

northern view that the mass of people in the South
had been misled, and that they were victims of superior minds, not wilful rebels. Their leaders
were the ones to be punished; they themselves
were to be forgiven. The best answer to this
theory was made by Henry Ward Beecher in the
Christian Union:

"We hold this view," he wrote in the issue of
May 1, 1872, "to be a mistaken one. We think it
is wrong, first, in assuming that the rebellion *was*
the work of a few conspirators. No half-dozen
men, no hundred or thousand men, carried the
South into rebellion. The ship was steered by a
few, but the engine that moved it was a whole
class—the flower and strength of the southern
people. It was the young men, the editors, the
lawyers, the politicians, who gave the impulse.
And the southern politicians were not the same
class as with us. Politics was the natural occupation of the southern gentlemen. The most active,
intelligent, enthusiastic element in the whole population, the element that naturally leads and
dominates in every crisis, originated and carried
out the idea of secession. Jefferson Davis was no
more the author of the rebellion than Abraham
Lincoln was the author of loyalty. Each gave
head to a cause where millions gave heart and
hand."

Mr. Beecher added truly: "What does this exclusion of a few thousand from office amount to,

as a terror to would-be rebels hereafter? If we meant to do that, we should have punished in another fashion. We should have hanged every officer in the rebel army and confiscated every acre owned by a rebel. We should have disfranchised the white population and put the country under military government for a century. Why did we not do it? Was it weakness or sentimentality that constrained us? Was it pity and magnanimity? It is none of these, but a simple sense of justice that keeps a Christian country from such a course. It was recognition of the fact that the southern people deserved no such treatment, that stayed our hand when the war was ended. These eight million people were not criminals. They had made a terrible mistake. They had fought in a bad cause. And for that, they had already paid a fearful penalty. But they were honest and brave people. They were worthy to be American citizens."

His conclusion was most sound. He said: "This exclusion policy is worse than locking the door after the horse is stolen. It is locking the door against the horse's return. Because a part of our citizens have been disloyal, we are taking pains to keep them so."

The army at the moment consisted of 56,815 men, of whom something like twenty-one thousand were quartered in the South. It must be said that the generals placed over the five districts acted with discretion. The peril of the period did not come from them, but from the wretched state governments which they were compelled to sustain. Sheridan was the least tactful. He had not yet got over the fighting spirit. Louisiana was also the most difficult of all the states to handle. For another thing, the carpetbaggers found it impossible to succeed at either cotton-growing or in business. This led to economic distress, always a bad concomitant for political dissension. Native southerners who took sides with the newcomers, were pleasantly called "scalawags." Here enters the Ku Klux Klan.

This secret organization, which was to breed so much trouble for the country, both during reconstruction and by revival half a century later, had its origin in an idle freak of half a dozen young ex-Confederates living at Pulaski, Tennessee. On December 24, 1865, or soon after the close of the war, they met in the law office of Thomas M. Jones, and at the suggestion of John C. Lester formed a club to break the drab dullness of their lives. The others were John B. Kennedy, Frank D. McCord, Calvin G. Jones, Richard R. Reed and James R. Crowe. A week later the organization was perfected, Kennedy suggesting that the Greek word "kuklos," meaning circle, be adopted. Lester thought, as they were all of Scotch descent, the word "clan" should be added and offhand used "Ku Klux Klan," for the first time. It was unanimously adopted and mischief was soon on foot. The fancy proved easy to embellish. To enhance the mystery, Crowe evolved a uniform out of sheets and pillow-cases, a form of masquerade long popular in the land. Then borrowing some horses, the Klansmen rode solemnly through the village streets, calling on all the girls they knew, but making no sound of any sort.

Quite naturally, the episode roused interest in the dreary little place. Further to enhance the mystery, each man was sworn to secrecy. New members joined, and a headquarters was acquired in the house of Doctor Benjamin Carter, which had been half-wrecked by a cyclone. Frequent parades in costume, and growing numbers, caused a wave of fear to permeate the colored population, which had been enjoying unlimited idleness under emancipation. Almost automatically, the Africans began to work. Rumors of the miracle and the cause spread to the surrounding country. Men thronged to the ruined Carter house seeking membership. A masked and mounted man turned them over to other maskers, and they were soon full-fledged members of the mysterious circle.

Meanwhile, the inventors, gleeful over the success of their prank, but not at all clear as to where it was leading, had created a fanciful governing body, including a Grand Cyclops, a Grand Magi, a Grand Turk, Grand Scribe, Lictors and Night Hawks. Individual members were delightfully termed Ghouls. That this nonsense should breed a great and powerful organization is not so strange as may appear at first glance.

The evil consequences of war do not fall alone upon the conquered. Both sides bear them in differing proportions, with varied effects. To the vanquished, come poverty and despair; to the victors, inflation, deflation, speculation and economic demoralization, with industrial disturbances that afflict wage-earners and make the value of capital uncertain. Readjustment is slow in coming and usually requires a period of distress to find bottom. This is doubly true in cases of civil conflict.

When the strife between North and South ended with the surrender of General Robert E. Lee's army, April 9, 1865, problems at once arose, more difficult to compass than those of war. Nearly three-quarters of a million men who had marched under the Stars and Bars returned to their homes unfit for any trade but fighting, their minds so filled with the great events in which they had shared as to make it difficult for all but a very few to face realities. There was no industry to enter save that of agriculture, hitherto in the hands of slaves. These were now free, but bewildered, with no longing to take up loads, and no intelligence with which to act for themselves. Slavery had been more of a liability than an asset. It had piled up no capital. The people had the productive soil, but no money. The thing most needed was a common starting point. This could not be found.

THE DREADFUL DECADE

In the North, the victors had nearly two million ex-soldiers on their hands, equally demoralized and equally adventurous. They could not, and did not, settle down. For many of these, however, there was an outlet. The government, most unwisely, threw away its greatest asset, the boundless lands of the West, in grants to soldiers and railroads, so stimulating a movement of new settlers that was not needed, and which reacted cruelly upon those who were tempted to partake. There were further unfortunate developments attending this policy. It stripped the New England States of young men, in addition to those who had died on the battle-field, and then began the tale of abandoned farms and stationary villages, in one of the hitherto fairest regions of our land. The "veterans" who stayed at home were inclined to spend their lives seeking office and pensions, few performing any useful service to their communities.

Unlike the South, however, the North gave opportunity to immigrants. These poured in. Varied industries gave them employment. There was no social disgrace attached to manual labor; no black semi-serviles to compete with. So cities grew around factories, and the inheritance of the Pilgrims fell to foreigners, while the true heirs sweated and suffered on the wind-swept plains, plagued by grasshoppers, tornadoes and mortgage sharks. The condition in the South was very different. Her soldiers were barred from the free lands, and at home all was forlorn. For two-thirds of its existence her politicians had controlled the government at Washington. During the anti-bellum period she had raised cotton, slaves and gentlemen of leisure. The poor whites were, and still remained, a negligible force. The aristocratic oligarchy was just as much in control as before the war, but, being disfranchised, had to seek some avenue other than political to work its ends. The Klan provided this.

When the civil conflict closed, the North possessed twenty-six states. Eleven in the South were conquered territory, without civil rights and no certainty as to their future political fate. The states of Delaware, Maryland, Missouri and Kentucky had never seceded, but many of their able-bodied men had fought with the Confederacy. During the period of revolt, Kansas and Nevada had been added to the Union, and a new commonwealth, West Virginia, composed of an area where most of the people were loyal, had been formed from a rib of the Mother of Presidents. Nevada was a sage-brush desert for the most part, with the population of a fourth-class city, but its two senators were often needed to perfect a two-thirds vote. The other Northern States were Maine, Vermont, New Hampshire, Rhode Island, Massachusetts, Connecticut, New York, Pennsylvania, Ohio, Indiana, Illinois, Wisconsin, Michigan, Minnesota, Iowa, Oregon and California. The territory under conquest comprised Virginia, North and South Carolina, Georgia, Florida, Tennessee, Alabama, Louisiana, Mississippi, Arkansas and Texas. Texas was a vast region with a scanty population; Arkansas, thinly settled and difficult of access; Florida had few people. The main impulse of the Klan was therefore found in the Carolinas, Georgia, Alabama, Louisiana and Mississippi, the most obdurate states in the late Confederacy.

It is by no means certain that there was not an underlying sentiment in the South for armed resistance to the rigors of northern rule. While it has been said with great stress on behalf of the Ku Klux Klansmen that they were organized for purely protective purposes, against local conditions, the fact that the organization soon had a wide membership made it take on a deeper meaning. The deposed oligarchy of the South saw in it a means to an end: Through it they could reconstruct their political power. Further than this, however, they preserved a considerable percentage of military might by selecting General Nathan Bedford Forrest as head of the Klan. When his name was brought up in the council at the Maxwell House, in Nashville, Tennessee, in May, 1867, (where they met secretly in Room No. 10) as the man to head the entire body, the crowd greeted him in unison as Wizard of the Saddle, with the result that Major James R. Crowe nominated him as Grand Wizard of the southwide Klan, thus injecting this title into the workings of the organization.

It chanced that General Robert E. Lee had been invited to attend this secret meeting, but declined. He had approved of the idea, but thought the Klan should keep itself "invisible." This caused the term Invisible Empire to be made the domain of the Grand Wizard. General Forrest was provided with ten assistant Wizards called Genii, and the whole South was districted into Realms, which in turn were partitioned into Dominions, a "dominion" being a congressional district. These were further divided into Provinces (which were counties) while the lesser divisions became Dens. Thus it will be seen, a wide and powerful organization was perfected. Under the silly name of Dragons (who governed Realms) and Hydras (who were the assistants) the management took local form. Grand Titans ruled the Dominions, while the chief of each Den was a Grand Cyclops, whose helpers were Night Hawks.

It seems incredible that grown men should have lent themselves to such nonsense and its incidental masquerading. But on reflection it will be seen that they were not men, but boys at heart still, as they were when they went blithely into the war.

Their elders took advantage of the appeal made by the horse-play and soon had an extraordinary control. They put themselves in a position to balk all moves affecting the government and the rights of the negroes. General John B. Gordon, of Georgia, became Forrest's right-hand man. Other strong and active supporters were John T. Morgan and James L. Pugh, of Alabama, James Z. George, of Mississippi, and Zebulun B. Vance, of North Carolina. Pugh was Grand Titan of Alabama, and Morgan, Grand Dragon. It might be added that all of these eminent gentlemen became United States senators and served with great credit. Apologists hold that all of them went into the Klan to restrain it, a statement that will not hold water. They went into it to use it, and did so, most successfully.

Some others who went in were sentimentalists. One was Father Abram J. Ryan, the poet-priest, who became Grand Chaplain of the Order, and General Albert Pike, of Arkansas, who was made Chief Justice.

One of the humors of the Klan period and its regulation of the negroes, befell Forrest. He was keenly desirous of securing a railroad from Selma, Alabama, to Memphis, Tennessee. The favorite method of financing such enterprises was by state and county loans, which led to some doleful debts. Lowndes County, Mississippi, through which the line was to run, was appealed to for a bond issue. The white planters were opposed to the plan, but Forrest, making use of the newly enfranchised black vote, carried the day. The whites took the matter to the United States Supreme Court. Forrest was defeated, and the road did not materialize.

Besides "regulating" their neighborhoods, the Klansmen erected and operated hidden cotton-gins in remote spots, thereby evading the federal tax which took much of the profits of the crop during the period of its enforcement. They contrived to market this contraband cotton in secret ways and so added to their scanty supply of cash.

The sign manual of the Klan was the fiery cross. Commands were dated from headquarters of the Realm: Dreadful Era, Black Epoch. The Ritual was never put into type, but recited by word of mouth and then subscribed to.

Parson W. G. Brownlow, Reconstruction Governor of Tennessee, was the first to move legislatively against the Klan. He was bitter toward the ex-Confederates and caused the passage of an act under which state troops were several times sent out to restore order in rebellious counties. Five years' imprisonment and fines as high as twenty thousand dollars were authorized.

The Ku Klux situation became so acute that Congress, on April 7, 1871, appointed a joint committee of House and Senate to look into its activities and report. Furthermore, Congress passed a severe measure that became a law on April 20, 1871, under which the president could suspend the right of habeas corpus and deal with conditions as he saw fit. This he did only once in nine South Carolina counties on October 17, 1871, having previously issued a warning proclamation. It had a calming effect on the Klan, though under the act many arrests were made, and men sent to federal prisons.

In a letter to Gerrit Smith, Henry B. Stanton, husband of Elizabeth Cady Stanton, pointed out that "an act to enforce the provisions of the Fourteenth Amendment," as the measure was entitled, "had no such powers," as these were not included in the amendment itself. The only effect from it would be to bring the Constitution into disrepute, which was precisely what happened. He prophesied in a word of warning that the amendments would be wiped out by such abuse in their name—which has long since become true. "If," he said, "one third of the Southern States are to be declared in rebellion, and, under suspension of the habeas corpus, persons who commit crimes against their local laws, are, by authority of the president, to be tried at the drumhead and imprisoned or shot, according to martial law, it will be done on some other pretext than that of enforcing the amendments."

The investigating committee dug away at the subject until February 19, 1872, summoning witnesses from all over the South, among them General Forrest, who came before it at Washington, June 22, 1871. General Forrest blandly disclaimed all knowledge of, or connection with, the Klan. He was mildly deprecatory and, as one correspondent put it, was the last man any one would be likely to take for the great Confederate cavalryman. He kept his share in the Invisible Empire quite in the dark and explained at some length his efforts to build the Selma railroad as proof of his attitude toward Africans.

The report, a large volume, with twelve hundred pages of printed testimony, was presented by the majority made up of the Republican members. It characterized the Klan as a political body intent upon restoring the power of the Democrats. Numerous outrages were cited. The report held that while the Klan was lawless before the Reconstruction Act was passed, it became virile and pestiferous after that piece of legislation went into effect. That most of the state governments were bad, it maintained, was due to the refusal of the wealthy and educated to do their part. No testimony was taken concerning Klan activities in Virginia, Tennessee, Arkansas, Louisiana and Texas. The Democratic minority, led by James B. Beck, of Kentucky, held that the Klan was sporadic in its activities and was in no sense a southwide body. The admitted wrong-doing, they claimed, was mere local disorder, to be dealt with according to state statutes. But behind this minimizing, they bulked the southern grievances. Negroes could bear arms and parade in uniform; white men could not. In short, their inferiors enjoyed rights which southern whites were denied, and their resentment was reasonable, even if their acts were evil. Conditions improved momentarily, and in taking office for his second term, March 4, 1873, Grant reported the lessening of lawlessness in the South as a happy augury.

The president saw the wisdom of removing political disabilities, and urged accordingly in his message of December 4, 1871. The House, at its previous session, had passed such a measure, but it had been halted in the Senate. Lyman Trumbull, of Illinois, tried to expedite it at the new session, but Senator Sumner insisted on tying to it a Civil Rights Bill prohibiting all forms of discrimination against negroes; getting his bill over by Vice-President Colfax's breaking a tie. The Democrats, refusing to link the two, helped to kill amnesty. Benjamin F. Butler put a measure through the House in March, independent of Civil Rights, and it passed the Senate in May, with but two votes against it. One of these was Sumner's. He thought they should be just to negroes before they were generous to rebels. The bill restored the rights of all but a few hundred of the leading southern whites, who remained proscribed. It became a law, May 22, 1872. The South had begun to fill seats in the Senate and House, and special acts removed the disabilities of distinguished men as they came up for preferment. The anti-Ku

Klux law expired by limitation in 1872, and an effort to extend it to March 4, 1873, failed. Thus, slowly, reason took the place of partisanship.

The so-called "carpetbag" governors were not, as might be supposed, all transplantations from the North who came down to aggrandize upon the conquered. Franklin J. Moses, Jr., of South Carolina, the worst of the lot, was among the Confederate forces at Charleston when Sumter was fired upon. He was a native of the state and of Hebrew descent. He had been speaker of the reconstruction legislature and notoriously corrupt in that office. The legislature was black and bad-white in composition. It voted all sorts of extravagances, including one thousand dollars to reimburse the speaker for a lost wager. For four years (1868 to 1872) R. K. Scott was governor. He was an immigrant from Ohio. Moses succeeded him for two years and brought the proud commonwealth to a low estate. Both Scott and his successor sold pardons and privileges. They piled debt upon the state, for which it received little or no return. Their period was one of debauch and dishonesty. The Mother of the Rebellion was made to suffer sorely for her sins.

Daniel H. Chamberlain, a lawyer from Massachusetts, had been attorney-general under Governor Scott, and the negro vote put him in as successor to Moses, who lived afterward mainly by his wits. Chamberlain was a man of character, who

[37]

did the best he could with the poor material given him by his party. He was the last of his kind.

The reconstruction governor of North Carolina was W. W. Holden, editor of the *Raleigh Standard,* who had shown the courage to call for peace and the downfall of Jefferson Davis in the midst of the war, for which his office was wrecked. His friends retaliated by spilling the type used to produce the "Secesh" *State Journal.* Andrew Johnson made him provisional governor, and he was elected later, taking office July 4, 1868. Though a native, he allowed the new elements to work their will, perhaps in vengeance for his own treatment. He soon clashed with the Ku Klux and was given a regiment of regulars to uphold his brand of law and order. The mountain tribes, who had been drafted and harried during the war, were behind him. Resisted, he declared Caswell and Alamance Counties in a state of insurrection, which was nothing new for the latter. Its "regulators" had risen against oppressive authority a century before. Holden's action brought out a statewide protest. His militia were mountain whites commanded by Colonel G. W. Kirk, who made many arrests and aroused fear of summary courts-martial and military executions. The national troops quartered at Raleigh were negroes. This added to the hatreds of the hour, caste and class being in collision. Holden controlled the courts and these refused relief. Habeas corpus proceedings in the United States District Court brought Kirk's captives within the national jurisdiction, which caused Holden to appeal to Grant to support him by shifting the custody of the prisoners to the United States marshal, who could call upon the regulars in the event of need. Grant referred the question to his attorney-general, A. T. Akerman, who sustained the action of the court. The prisoners were released. At the election which followed (1870), the state went Democratic. This quelled the insurrection and gave the legislature to the Democrats. Holden was impeached for his proclamation, convicted and ousted from office. Besides creating trouble, he had managed to increase the state debt from sixteen million dollars to twice that sum.

No one lent more heat to the combat than Albion W. Tourgee, of Ohio, a soldier who settled in Greensboro, North Carolina, after the war and was elected judge of the Superior Court, serving until 1874. His district included the Ku Klux counties of the state, and his difficulties were many. An able man, but intensely partisan, he fitted badly into his surroundings. When his term as judge expired, he was made collector of internal revenue, an uncomfortable job in a land of "moonshine." He subsequently wrote a book about his adventures in North Carolina, *A Fool's Errand, by One of the Fools,* which had a wide circulation when issued in 1879. It served as a valuable argument for the bloody-shirt wavers in the campaign of 1880. The volume was in the form of a novel and very well written. Tourgee was an honest man but helpless and miserable in menacing surroundings. Most northern men who went South before the war became more southern than the southerners, while those who went after the war did not.

Virginia, whose vote for secession had given the Civil War a status which it could not have otherwise attained, and bore the brunt of the conflict, came lightly out of the reconstruction turmoil. Near the center of government, with a smaller negro problem than several of her sister states, she was soon rehabilitated. For one thing, the state was in Major-General John M. Schofield's military district, and he exercised great wisdom in dealing with affairs. By his action no carpetbagger was installed at the head of the government, though a good many got into minor offices. At a special election in July, 1869, Gilbert C. Walker, a Conservative, was elected, and with him, a legislature of the same stripe. They did not take control until January 1, 1870, on which date senators and representatives from Virginia were allowed to assume their seats. Texas kept Virginia company, passing through the period of reconstruction with comparatively little turmoil.

Alabama was treated to a negro legislature and

was one of the first states "redeemed" by the radicals. A riot followed the meeting of her new
legislature. Her governor, W. H. Smith (Republican), was not corrupt but careless. He was
succeeded by a Democrat who was no improvement, which led to another Republican victory in
1872, David P. Lewis becoming governor. He
required a company of United States Cavalry to
seat his legislature and gave the state two years
of carpetbag rule of the most improved kind. He
was routed by George S. Houston, at the election
in 1874, with the help of the Ku Klux, who were
intensely active. Many outrages were justly laid
to their credit against both white and black
Republicans. Sumter, Russell, Coffee, Pickens,
Marengo and Choctaw Counties were the scenes of
the chief disturbances. The atrocities were exag-
gerated for purposes of political capital and made
the subject of much oratory in Congress. Although the governor, a Republican, did not ask it,
Grant sent a regiment of regulars to the state to
supervise the election in 1874. In spite of this,
the Democrats won. Congress investigated the
election by a committee, the Republican majority
of which held that the election had been won by
fraud and violence, but the House did not bother
itself further about the matter. Alabama remained
"solid" ever after.

Georgia had been reconstructed early, thanks
to the military adjustment of her legislature, which

gave it enough negro votes to accept the amendments and so elected R. B. Bullock as governor, defeating General John B. Gordon. Bullock was only constructively a carpetbagger. He had come to Georgia before the war to develop telegraph and railway enterprises, of which he became the head, and espoused the Confederacy. With Hannibal I. Kimball, a man from Norway, Oxford County, Maine, he took hold of the rebuilding of Atlanta, burned by Sherman, and worked hard to restore the railroads and industry. The legislature, being propped up by bayonets, was certain to change its complexion at the next election. Bullock therefore plotted brazenly to keep it in power by an act of Congress, and the necessary bill was introduced by Benjamin F. Butler. It extended the life of the body two years, or to 1872. The Senate could not swallow this, and expressed the opinion that the legislature as it stood was illegal. Bullock's efforts in the lobby completed the defeat of the scheme. Three-fourths of the states had now ratified the Fifteenth Amendment, so the secretary of state proclaimed its adoption as the law of the land on March 30, 1870. Congress now gave Georgia a right to hold its election.

A Democratic legislature was elected, but the carpetbag Senate holding over decreed that it should not meet until 1872, all hands in office staying on until then. This did not work. To the credit of the president, he lent no aid to Bullock in his dishonest schemes to retain power. Bullock was charged with corruption and mismanagement of the state-owned railroad running from Atlanta to Chattanooga. Either in disgust, or feeling that the odds were too heavy, he resigned October 23, 1871, and left Georgia. This was considered a confession of guilt. Later, in 1876, when conditions were calmer, he came back to Atlanta, faced trial under indictment and was acquitted with a clean bill of moral health. He was succeeded as governor by Benjamin J. Conley, a Democrat, the president of the State Senate. At the special election which followed, James M. Smith was chosen governor. He, too, was a Democrat, as have been all the governors to follow him. Georgia was again in the hands of her own people.

Thanks to a negro legislature, Mississippi came in out of the cold in 1870, sending, as one of its senators, Major-General Adelbert Ames to Washington. He was Benjamin F. Butler's son-in-law, an offense in itself, but the control of the radicals continued, and he was made governor by election in 1874. The Ku Klux and White Leaguers now determined to restore home rule and became very troublesome during the campaign of 1875, riding over the country and intimidating the negroes. Ames was an amiable, well-meaning man, but could not sustain himself in his uneasy chair. Blacks were more numerous in his state than in any other, and the night riders began a

reign of terror. Rough frolics frightened the negroes away from political meetings, scared them
out of office and made their lives miserable. Yazoo
City, where the ram *Arkansas* had been built during the war, became the scene of a bloody conflict,
followed by a similar clash at Clinton. The governor called on President Grant for federal
troops, but the nearest soldiers had their hands full
in Louisiana, and Grant, whose opinion of Ames
was none too high, withheld them on an opinion
of Attorney-General Edwards Pierrepont that
none could be legally sent until it was plain that
the state's own resources were unequal to restoring
and preserving order. There could, of course, be
no reliance placed upon a white state militia in
Mississippi, and the blacks had become so intimidated that they were not eager to respond to the
emergency. The situation promised to insure the
coming of the regulars. This the better white
element did not care to see, knowing that it meant
a further delay in restoring their power. They
therefore made a deal with Ames that he should
not mobilize the negroes, in return for which they
agreed to make their compatriots behave. Ames,
therefore, did not call out the colored companies.
The last two weeks of the canvass were orderly,
but white supremacy showed thirty thousand majority at the polls.

This gave the control of the legislature to the
white element, which proceeded to clean house with

celerity. The lieutenant-governor and superintendent of education were impeached and removed
from office. Ames endeavored to stay the ener-
gies of his foes by proclaiming the new legislature
an illegal body, as being elected by violence and
fraud, which was no doubt true. The response of
the statesmen was to impeach His Excellency.
Rather than face trial, he agreed to resign on condition that the articles of impeachment be withdrawn. This proposal was accepted, and he
stepped out on March 26, 1876, to return to
Massachusetts, whence he came.

In Louisiana, the reconstruction problem
looked simple. Henry C. Warmoth, a carpetbagger from Illinois, became governor, and a legislature of mixed breeds passed the necessary
legislation to accord with the law. A plebiscite
endorsed this. Disabilities were removed, and all
would have gone well, but for a factional quarrel
that broke out among the new rulers in 1872.
Warmoth backed John McEnery for his successor
in the governor's chair, while the Republicans, as
they called themselves, got behind William P. Kellogg, whose sponsor was S. B. Packard, United
States Marshal. The conservative element, which
included such Democrats as cared to vote, supported McEnery. The final canvass of the votes
was made by a "returning board" which included
the governor, lieutenant-governor, secretary of
state and two non-officials. This board had

power to decide the validity of all votes cast and to judge of illegal interferences or oppositions at the polls. The result of the balloting was highly confusing. McEnery claimed ten thousand majority and Kellogg eighteen thousand. The returning board seated McEnery, but Packard, in addition to being United States marshal, with power to call on the regular troops under the Reconstruction Act, was chairman of the Republican state committee. He calmly appointed a returning board of his own, proclaimed Kellogg governor, seized the state-house with the support of Sheridan's soldiers and placed Kellogg in the governor's chair. Grant upheld Packard.

The affair was investigated by the United States Senate Committee on Privileges and Elections, which came to the conclusion that neither man ought to be governor. An effort to pass a bill to enforce a new election was defeated by Oliver P. Morton, and Kellogg was kept in office by the potent power of federal bayonets. There followed what amounted to civil war. Kellogg was tyrannical and corrupt. The people revolted, and turbulence coupled with armed resistance became the rule. Kellogg's judges were defied, and law enforcement was left mainly to "Judge Lynch." At Colfax, in Grant Parish, a small battle with many fatalities resulted. The sheriff, under orders from the governor, undertook to protect a judge who was not welcome. He raised a posse of black men and barricaded the court-house, throwing up earthworks to protect the approaches. The dispatches of the day say he then gathered five hundred men, who were soon assailed by one hundred and twenty-five armed whites.

On the sacred Sunday of Easter, April 13, 1873, the sheriff was called upon, under a flag of truce, to surrender the court-house and send his posse away. This he refused to do, and a fusillade followed. The garrison returned fire, but the colored soldiers were poor shots. Only two assailants were killed, but fifty-nine of the luckless defenders were slain. All were negroes, and the affair added to the terrors of their lot. This was followed by a clash at St. Martinsville, where the federal troops interfered before anything serious happened. The blacks armed themselves all through the troubled sections, while the whites organized a White League, which openly operated against Kellogg. There were no masks or Ku Klux monkey-shines in their performances. Six offensive Kellogg officers were forced to resign in Coushatta on the Red River after numbers of men, black and white, had been killed. The deposed officials were butchered while presumably under safe conduct en route from Shreveport.

In the interest of peace, President Grant removed the scattered garrisons, leaving only a small federal force at New Orleans. This proved to be a mistake. Following the fashion of their

French forebears, the citizens barricaded the streets on September 14, 1874, and resisted the efforts of the police to clear the way. The latter were mainly negroes and suffered severely in the fighting. Each side had a number killed—about twenty or more, in all—but the White Leaguers were victorious. They captured the state-house and organized a provisional government.

Grant sent the soldiers back and reestablished Kellogg on his shaky throne in time to have that gentleman supervise the fall election at which a legislature was to be chosen. An anti-Kellogg majority was the result on the face of the returns. The governor's returning board gave each side fifty-three out of one hundred and eleven and left five seats open, having apparently exhausted their rascality. This brought Congress into the situation and a sub-committee—Charles Foster, of Ohio, William Walter Phelps, of New Jersey, Republicans, and Clarkson N. Potter, of New York, Democrat—were sent to New Orleans. Their investigation produced a report adverse to Kellogg. Packard was found to have grossly abused his office by the use of soldiers and deputy marshals, who were plenty at the polls, while the returning board's actions were absolutely rascally. Negroes were found to have been illegally registered to overcome the overplus of whites. In New Orleans, fifty-two hundred such cases were disclosed.

While the sub-committee was in the city the time came to organize the legislature. The White

RECONSTRUCTION

League men took control and elected **L. B. Wiltz** speaker, on January 5, 1875. Proceeding to business, they seated five conservatives in the seats left undecided by Kellogg's board, whereupon sundry Republicans started to withdraw to break the quorum. On order of the speaker, they were stopped by the sergeant-at-arms. Tumult arising, Wiltz called for soldiers. These came under command of General Regis de Trobriand who proceeded to take matters into his own hands by expelling the five conservatives, an utterly unwarranted proceeding.

Upon this, Wiltz and his following withdrew, and the other side took possession. Sheridan had come to town and gave signs of exercising a high hand. He wrote Grant that the people were "banditti," and suggested the arrest and trial of the White League leaders as a cure for the terrorism that undoubtedly prevailed. Grant indorsed Sheridan, but the public did not, nor did Foster's committee. Carl Schurz led the protest in the Senate. The president was called upon for information and gave it, holding that Sheridan had "never proposed to do an illegal act," which was true. He had merely asked for a law that would legalize the acts he proposed. Foster's committee made its report on January fifteenth. It was unanimous and forceful. The effect was politically refreshing, but disconcerting to the partisans in Congress, who sent an all-Republican committee to New Orleans. Its members were George F. Hoar, of Massachu-

[49]

setts, William P. Frye, of Maine, and William A. Wheeler, of New York. These gentlemen reported to Congress on February 23, 1875. Hoar wrote the report. It reeked with a record of "outrages." They could not prove, however, that the election had been other than legal. The outcome was the return of the conservatives into control of the legislature with a majority of twelve. Under this compromise, Kellogg remained governor, and the diverse elements held each other at bay until the election of 1876.

In discussing the giving of the franchise to negroes William P. Frye, later United States senator, once said to me: "It was a great and terrible mistake. But what else could we do? We had just won a great war and the South, coming back full white, meant the loss of our party's power, so we did as we did. I had as much to do with it as anybody. But it was a great and terrible mistake."

The Ku Klux Klan formally mustered itself out of existence at Athens, Alabama, in a private hall maintained in the mansion of Henry J. Pepin, early in September, 1877. Forrest, still its head, was very ill and near his end. He summoned the Grand Dragons into a solemn conclave and formally released them from their oaths. The Invisible Empire had passed away. In the eyes of the South it has become glorified, while in strange contrast its revived prototype has gained its greatest strength in the North.

[50]

CHAPTER II

FISK AND GOULD

Pupils of Cornelius Vanderbilt and Daniel Drew, Inventors of High Finance—The Capture of Erie—Their Effort to Corner Gold—Black Friday—The Orange Riot—Murder of Fisk.

THE beginning of the era of railway wrecking as a source of wealth-making had its inception on the eighth of October, 1867, when the demon, chance, brought James Fisk, Jr., and Jay Gould together for the first time. Both were young, Fisk having been born at Pownal, Vermont, April 1, 1835, and Gould at Roxbury, Delaware County, New York, May 27, 1836. Fisk's career had already been florid; Gould's had been that of a cat in a corner. Son of a Vermont peddler operating out of Brattleboro with horse and cart, Fisk had "cut his eye-teeth," as the Yankees say, very early. When a husky boy he left home and traveled for seven years with Van Amburgh's circus, a great school for sophistication; returning with a large supply of this quality, he took over his father's trade routes in the Green Mountains. But, unlike the elder, he went at it circus fashion. Four splendid horses, clad in silver-mounted harness, drew a great van, gaily painted and decorated with pic-

[51]

tured panels executed in the highest style of the
then elegant coachmaker's art. His own person
was equal to these trappings. He was a handsome
blond young fellow who made a strong appeal to
the wizened females of his territory, and this quality, along with showy wares, brought great prosperity to the outfit.

Dealing with the wholesale department of a
Boston dry-goods house, Jordan Marsh Company,
his large transactions excited the attention of its
shrewd head, Eben D. Jordan, who proceeded to
annex the enterprising young man. His business
was purchased at a round price, and he was taken
care of with a salesman's position in the Boston
shop. The Civil War came on, and the firm, having on hand a large supply of blankets, sent the
new man to Washington to work them off on the
government. This he did with great profit, and
established such relations with the quartermaster's
department as to bring his firm much business. He
also scented out a fabric mill at Gaysville, Vermont, the purchase of which gave the house a
monopoly of material much used at the time.
These achievements led to an interest in the firm.
When New Orleans fell into federal hands, April
25, 1862, Fisk went South to pick up cotton for the
Jordan Marsh mills. He had many adventures,
including the destruction by explosion of ammunition of their steamer *Joseph Pierce,* involving a loss of three hundred and fifty thousand

Col. James Fisk, Jr.

dollars. It had been commandeered by troops and was blown up soon after they took possession. The government would never pay the bill.

Fisk made his father an associate in the risky game, but a stroke of apoplexy disabled the senior and sent him, mentally incompetent, to a sanitarium. Fisk outrode all his storms and was so much a factor that Jordan felt it would be safer to do business without him. He was retired, with two hundred and fifty thousand dollars for his interest, and set up a store on Chauncey Street that lost money too rapidly for comfort. Fisk closed out and departed for New York to try his luck, with what cash remained, on the New York Stock Exchange. That bewitching institution soon emptied his pockets, and he returned to Boston to refresh his stake.

Jordan evidently helped him to return. He came back wiser, however, resolving to become a "broker," rather than a "customer," and with one William Belden established a stock shop at 37 Broad Street, under the firm name of Fisk, Belden and Company. Belden was a man of little character and less consequence. Here he "got along," as the saying is, until the fortunate October eighth.

Gould's story was simpler, but along lines of venture, too. He began his career early. As a fifteen-year-old boy he had got up a map and history of Delaware County, which he sold himself, tramping among the back hills of the Catskills in search of buyers. Inventing an ingenious mouse-trap, he brought it to New York for market and saw a chance for larger game in Wall Street. Here he began to set traps as head of the firm of Smith, Gould, Martin and Company, at 11 Broad Street.

Up to the October date mentioned, it is not known that the young men had more than a casual acquaintance with each other if any, though near neighbors on the same thoroughfare.

While Wall Street has earned invidious repute as a center of lamb-shearing, much wool has been collected in State Street, Boston, with closer cutting and smoother clipping. There was floating around in 1866 a nebulous railway enterprise called the Boston, Hartford and Erie, presumed to run from the Hub to Fishkill, on the east bank of the Hudson, whence it connected by ferry with the branch of the Erie ending at Newburgh. Some two hundred and forty miles of single track existed, with a dozen locomotives and a few cars, trying to earn returns on twenty million dollars, besides taking care of the interest on ten kinds of mortgages representing as many millions of funded debt. As the road was of no account by itself, the State Street gentlemen conceived the bright idea of unloading some of its responsibilities on the Erie. John S. Eldridge was president of the concern. Daniel Drew, an old cattle dealer of Carmel, Putnam County, New York, had just finished trimming Commodore Cornelius Vanderbilt in a duel over control of the Erie. The Erie was the rival to the Great Lakes of Vanderbilt's newly perfected New York Central and Hudson River road, and he plotted revenge. He held a considerable interest in Erie and could always get more on Wall Street. The Boston crowd also had a heavy block of stock. The two interests got together, made a deal whereby the Erie guaranteed the interest on four million dollars of the Boston, Hartford and Erie bonds and at the annual meeting on October 8, 1867, they unhorsed Drew, elected John S. Eldridge president of the Erie, with a board of directors that included John S. Eldridge, Eben D. Jordan, Joseph Bardwell and James S. Whitney, of Boston; J. C. Bancroft Davis, Alexander S. Diven, Killiam Evans, James Fisk, Jr., Jay Gould, Dudley S. Gregory, George M. Graves, Frederick A. Lane, Homer Ramsdell, William B. Skidmore, Henry Thompson, Lewis Underwood and Frank Work. Work was Vanderbilt's broker. Underwood had been lieutenant-governor of Vermont and was also Vanderbilt's man. Henry Thompson was Eldridge's brother-in-law. Homer Ramsdell represented a considerable amount of Newburgh capital,

The assumption is fair that Eben D. Jordan was responsible for Fisk's place on the board. The backing for Gould is not visible in any attainable record. But they were now momentarily together.

[55]

The defeated Drew began taking account of stock and, to seek vengeance on the "victorious Corneel," as he called him, cunningly put into the hands of Fisk, Belden and Company the unloading of the Narragansett Steamship Company, now, and long, the famous Fall River line. Fisk handled this with such skill that he not only aided Drew, but came out of it with the control of the line and one million dollars in his pockets.

Events now moved fast. The eager Drew took on Fisk and Gould as active agents and between them they trapped Vanderbilt, the pair in the meantime having worked out a plan of their own.

Under the Eldridge management, though strongly intrenched, the commodore did not control, and Drew, anxious to regain his property, aided and abetted Fisk and Gould in their yet unrevealed scheme to get it themselves.

By negotiations with the Michigan Central and Canada Southern, arrangements were being made to lay a third rail on their standard-gauge tracks so as to give the Erie a broad-gauge line to Chicago. This meant serious competition for Vanderbilt's New York Central. He therefore sought to mix further in Erie affairs, and by using William M. Tweed's judge, George G. Barnard, he scored an advantage. Barnard enjoined Drew from acting as treasurer of the Erie and by a further order prohibited the issuing of more stocks and bonds. Drew was also commanded to restore to the company fifty-eight thousand shares of stock deviously acquired. Unappalled, Drew moved the company's offices to Jersey City, and from this vantage ground secured the authorization of a ten-million-dollar bond issue that could be converted into stock. This he did at once, giving half to Fisk and Gould. The other half Uncle Daniel fed to Wall Street, mainly to the Vanderbilt crowd, almost producing a panic. It was only prevented by the Exchange refusing to recognize shares dated after March 7, 1868.

Judge Barnard issued a threat that he would hold the Erie directors in five hundred thousand dollars bail each, if caught—which they were not. Drew now procured from Judge Ranson Balcom, sitting at Cortland, New York, an order forbidding Frank Work, Vanderbilt's director in the Erie, from sitting in the board on the ground that his presence as a New York Central factor was inimical to the welfare of the road. Vanderbilt retorted with an order from Judge Ingraham forbidding the Erie board to transact any business unless Work was present. Drew next secured an order from Judge Jasper W. Gilbert, in Brooklyn, commanding the Erie directors to do business without Work. The whole tangle came up before Judge George G. Barnard on March 10, 1868, but as neither side knew how to proceed, the hearing went over until the fourteenth.

Barnard then appointed George A. Osgood

[57]

receiver. He was Vanderbilt's son-in-law and a personal friend of the judge. The Erie exiles procured an order from Judge Clerke, sitting in Ulster County, forbidding the receiver to act. Ordered to appear in this matter before Barnard, they secured an even more sweeping order from Judge Clerke, which thoroughly tied Barnard's hands, though he attempted to make Osgood's appointments effective. An appeal was taken from Clerke's order, but Judge Ingraham granted a writ restraining Osgood, pending the result. After a hearing before the General Term, Judges Barnard, Cardozo and Ingraham sitting, the appeal was sustained by vote of Cardozo and Barnard, the latter having in the interim appointed Peter B. Sweeny as receiver in place of Osgood!

In the meantime, the Fisk-Gould-Drew crowd secured an act from the New Jersey Legislature legalizing their stock issues and other performances and sought the same thing in New York. While in Albany pressing this legislation, Jay Gould was arrested on Judge Barnard's order, but gave bail and was never haled to court for his share in the lurid financing. He remained in Albany until the bill was passed, which it was, amid much scandal, the Vanderbilt interests giving way.

Bewildering as all this seems, it is easily made clear. Fisk and Gould behind the scenes perceived the need of taking the judicial and legislative power away from Vanderbilt. They saw that

it was exercised by William M. Tweed and Peter
B. Sweeny, of the celebrated Tammany ring, then
newly risen to power. The pair had been working
their influence for Commodore Vanderbilt. Incidentally, the commodore himself had innocently
supplied the key. In fighting Drew at Albany,
Tweed spent, so he claimed, one hundred and
eighty thousand dollars securing senatorial votes,
and for "security" received a big block of Vanderbilt's Erie shares. This opened the way for the
close connections established. In the settlement
that preceded his withdrawal from the fight, Commodore Vanderbilt, who held ten million dollars' worth, sold five millions of stock to the road
itself at seventy. Fisk and Gould then made a
contract to buy the balance in six months, paying
one million dollars for the "call." Through Fisk,
Belden and Company, they next sold one hundred
thousand shares "short," and broke the price from
seventy-two and one-half to thirty-five, shaking
out enough, with the five million dollars in the
treasury from the Vanderbilt purchase, to give
them control. The thirty-four million dollars capitalization was now increased to fifty-four million
dollars and Vanderbilt took forty dollars a share for
his remaining shares under the call. At the Erie
election held on October 13, 1868, John S. Eldridge
and Daniel Drew were dropped. Jay Gould became president and James Fisk, Jr., treasurer and
comptroller. William M. Tweed and Peter B.

Sweeny were added to the directorate. Sweeny never qualified and always claimed to have remained true to the Vanderbilt interests.

Tweed once explained the establishment of the relationship in this way:

In 1868, Mr. Tweed was brought into relations with Jay Gould by Mr. Hugh Hastings at the Delavan House, Albany. During the session of 1868, Mr. Tweed had no business connections with Mr. Gould, but, on the contrary, in behalf of the New York Central road, Mr. Tweed had opposed his measures.

After the adjournment, Mr. Gould asked permission to bring Mr. Fisk in contact with Mr. Tweed, and did bring him to Mr. Tweed's office. Mr. Tweed introduced Messrs. Gould and Fisk to Mr. Sweeny, who had been appointed receiver of the Erie Railway, contrary to their wishes.

In order to obtain control of the road again, an arrangement was made by which Mr. Sweeny was to receive, and did receive, one hundred and fifty thousand dollars for his fees, which amount was divided equally between Sweeny, Hugh Smith (Sweeny's agent) and Mr. Tweed.

From that time, all legislation desired by the Erie road was obtained by Mr. Tweed, and money expended for such purposes was defrayed by Gould and Fisk, and disbursed by Mr. Tweed, Mr. Barber and Abraham Van Vechten, under Mr. Tweed's direction.

Mr. Tweed says that one hundred thousand dollars was expended in this way. In consideration for these services of Mr. Tweed, he, Mr.

Sweeny and Hugh Smith were made directors of the road, although they owned no stock, and were given privileges in stock and other operations.

Mr. Tweed also brought Fisk in communication with Judge Barnard, who thereafter granted them all the judicial aid they required. Messrs. Gould and Fisk contributed handsomely to all election funds when requested so to do by the ring, and aided them all it was in their power to do, in connection with the road, to advance their political interests.

In Fisk, Tweed found a kindred soul. They stood together until the end.

As a sample effort on Fisk's and Gould's behalf, Tweed obligingly saw that Charles J. Folger was elected judge in their interests. Folger was a Republican, who at a later day was to bring disaster upon his party and become the means of making Grover Cleveland president of the United States. Tickets were made up, correctly printed as Democratic ballots, but the name Folger was substituted for one or another of the Democratic candidates in various wards, there being three vacancies. Sweeny, Connolly and Tweed fixed up the whole scheme. "This arrangement was entered into and consummated," wrote Tweed, "to oblige Mr. Gould, with whom the ring was then operating."

Fisk now gave up his broker's shop in Broad Street and blossomed out in splendor. Pike's Opera House, newly built, at Eighth Avenue and Twenty-third Street, was purchased, and the Erie installed there in gorgeous offices. It had done business in shabby quarters in Jersey City. The theater remained, elegantly refitted, as the Grand Opera House. The price paid for it was eight hundred and forty thousand dollars—an enormous sum for the day. There being some criticism of the transaction, Fisk bought it back, repaying the road with a bundle of its own moist stock and keeping it as a tenant at seventy-five thousand dollars rental per year. He imported stars from abroad and set up a seraglio. Gould kept him company, but not in dissipation. His mind was full of further schemes for financing Erie. Eldridge was brazenly prosecuted for wasting the company's money in buying legislation authorizing the stock-watering. The sum so squandered was set at five million dollars.

Joyous in triumphant rascality, Gould now set the stage for a nation-wide calamity. President Grant had taken office on March 4, 1869, and financial questions were foremost, stimulated always by the speculation in gold as against the value of the greenback. Fisk and Gould had made no advances on Washington during the Johnson era, the stealing of the Erie not requiring national help. But they found in the gold gambling an opportunity for renewed speculation and laid their wires to enmesh the president. On June 15, 1869, a great "Peace Jubilee" opened in Boston, in which Patrick Sarsfield Gilmore's brass band was launched as a national feature, while colossal choruses bawled songs of joy.

The president was invited to attend and was cleverly routed via the Narragansett Steamship Line, leaving New York on the evening of the fourteenth. He was accompanied by Cyrus W. Field and other eminent citizens, while Gould and Fisk took pains to be in evidence. The steamer *Providence*, gorgeously decorated from stem to stern, took the run that night. Fisk met the presidential party at the pier in his full panoply of an admiral's uniform, laden with gold lace. A bridal chamber was set apart for Grant's use, and champagne flowed in rivers for the company. Dodworth's famous band tooted melodiously. It must have been bewildering to the plain little man from the army. Fisk attached himself to the presidential party during its Boston stay, listened to the anvil, cannon and other charivari devised by the ingenious Gilmore, and was photographed with the attendant generals and admirals. Indeed, he came so near being the whole show as to have "Jubilee Jim" added to the "Prince of Erie."

In the midst of all this flurry, neither he nor Gould forgot their purpose, which was to find out how Grant stood on the subject of further contracting the currency. The little they elicited was not favorable to inflation, and Gould unloaded much of his gold. From a momentary high point of three hundred and ten it had settled down to one hundred and thirty, with a tendency to go lower. Indeed, the period of wild speculation showed signs of ending. The temptation to make a plunge was, however, too great to be resisted, and there now developed the most sensational episode of the era in an attempt on the part of Gould and Fisk to corner the supply of gold. The Stock Exchange had a gold room in which its members executed orders for the metal, both for legitimate customers, who needed it to pay their taxes to the Federal Government, and those who speculated in its fluctuations. Gould, on behalf of his railway interests, as he always contended, undertook to execute a corner that would elevate it to one hundred and forty-five.

The cunning young financier planned his plot with exemplary care. The trip with Grant suggested the way. First he took into his confidence Abel Rathbone Corbin, who had married General Grant's sister. He was a man of sixty-seven, who had made a good deal of money out of the relationship, and was in a position to retire. Again the simple soldier was taken on an excursion, this time to Newport, on August 5, 1869, Fisk in his uniform once more playing the host with lavish perfection. The pair found the general still impervious to inflation. He thought the gas ought to be let out some more, which by no means met with the views of the conspirators. Grant's instinct was to release the gold held in the Treasury—

some one hundred million dollars, and renew its use as currency. When he made this plain on the steamer, Gould gave it as his opinion that if such a policy were carried out, it would produce great distress and "almost lead to civil war." He added that strikes would follow among workmen, factories would close and business come to a halt. "I took the ground," he said later, when Congress inquired into the matter, "that the government ought to let gold alone, and let it find its commercial level; that, as a fact, it ought to facilitate an upward movement of gold in the fall."

Fisk, in telling his part of the story, said: "We went down to supper about nine o'clock, intending while we were there, to have this thing pretty thoroughly talked up, and, if possible, to relieve him (Grant) of any idea of putting the price of gold down; for, if his policy was such as to allow gold to go down to one hundred and twenty-five, our transportation would have been snapped right up. We talked there, I guess, until about half-past twelve. When he first began to talk, I could see that he was for returning to a specie basis. I remember the remark he made, that we might as well tap the bubble at once as any other time. He entered into the conversation with a good deal of spirit, and I made up my mind that he was individually paying a good deal of attention to the finances, which he would, to a certain extent, control."

This peril being clear, the pair now took pains to exert pressure that would enable them to carry out their scheme, and here began making use of Corbin, in whom was planted the idea that the business interests of the country required an advance in the price of gold; that in order to move the fall crops and secure a foreign market for the grain, it was requisite that the yellow metal should be put up to one hundred forty, and the greenback made that much cheaper. This inside influence was accentuated by an attempt to utilize the financial columns of the *New York Times,* of which John Bigelow was then, and briefly, the editor. On August 5, 1869, Bigelow had called on the president and the result was reflected in several editorials that purported to reveal his financial policy. Passing through New York on the nineteenth, Grant said nothing publicly on the subject, but the scamps used Corbin to write an article for the *Times* on "Grant's Financial Policy," which it purported to prove was to advance the price of gold. This was offered as an editorial, accepted, and put into type. Mr. Bigelow was not in the office, but the article came to his attention and he held it for the scrutiny of C. C. Norvel, the paper's financial editor. Norvel suspected something and revised the article into what he thought was nearer the real view of the administration, in which shape it was published on August twenty-sixth. It retained, however, the argument that the reduction in the

FISK AND GOULD

value of gold would effect a like loss on the value
of products, and this Gould seized upon in a letter
written to George S. Boutwell, Secretary of the
Treasury, on August thirtieth, which read:

Office of the Erie Railway Company,
President's Office, New York,
August 30, 1869.

My dear Sir: If the *New York Times* correctly reflects your financial policy during the next
three or four months, viz.: to unloose the currency
balance at the Treasury, or keep it at the lowest
possible figure, and also to refrain during the same
period from selling or putting gold on the market,
thus preventing a depression of the premium at a
season of the year when the bulk of our agricultural products have to be marketed, then I think
the country peculiarly fortunate in having a financial head who can take a broad view of the situation, and who realizes the importance of settling
the large balance of trade against us, by the extent
of our agricultural and mineral products, instead
of bonds and gold. You no doubt fully appreciate
the fact that in the export of breadstuffs to Euro-
pean markets, we have on our side high-priced
labor and long rail transportation to compete with
the cheap labor and water transportation of the
great grain-producing countries of the Black and
Mediterranean Seas, and it is only by making gold
high and scarce that the difference is equalized,
and we are enabled to compete in the London and
Liverpool markets. It is not merely the agricultural and producing classes all over the country,
north, west and south, that are enriched by your

[67]

policy of furnishing a foreign market for the surplus products of the country at good and remunerative prices, but as well the manufacturing and commercial interest. When the former classes are prosperous, they buy and consume liberally, thus bringing prosperity and wealth to the latter interest. This policy will also greatly benefit the vast railway interests—which can only prosper when the general business of the country is prosperous.

I sincerely believe that when the fruits of your policy come to be practically realized, all classes, the poor as well as the rich, will accord your services a generous appreciation.

With many apologies for thus troubling you, I remain, respectfully,

Yours,

JAY GOULD.

Hon. Geo. S. Boutwell,
Secretary of the Treasury, Washington, D. C.

Grant was influenced by the argument and wrote Boutwell that it would not be wise to sell the gold stock in "too large amounts," such as might force down the price while crops were moving. Boutwell, absent at his Massachusetts home, received this suggestion on September fourth, and telegraphed the Treasury not to part with any more gold. Fisk and Gould were fully informed of this by their inside agents, and the price of gold at once began to advance. They took care of Corbin by buying one million, five hundred thousand dollars in his name. General Daniel Butterfield had been appointed sub-treasurer in New York and he, too, was staked for a like sum, though he always insisted that it was done without his knowledge. By September sixth, the metal had risen to one hundred thirty-seven and one-half. Gould was the chief buyer. He bought all that was offered, but was surprised at the quantity. We had not been exporting much gold, and, as its value grew, Europe began to sell. This he had not anticipated. He swore at the inquiry that he had not intended to corner coin, but had to buy in order "not to show the white feather."

As a matter of fact, the "corner" was in process of creation. Gould and Fisk between them had been able to take all the gold offered, real and "phantom," as Fisk delightfully termed the short sales. They rested their faith on Corbin's assurance that the president would not order relief from the Treasury. That Corbin was selling an assurance he did not possess, is rather certain. Butterfield was kept in close touch—every fifteen minutes—during the hectic period, so that any word from Washington could be promptly acted upon. By September twenty-third, Gould had bought so much gold that he was not quite sure where he stood and called in Fisk. They became uneasy over the situation, and Fisk sought out Corbin at his house. Corbin, Fisk testified, told him that the president's wife had an interest of five hundred thousand dollars, that he, Corbin, held it, with one million, five hundred thousand dollars more, of which five hundred thousand dollars was for General Horace Porter, Grant's secretary. Fisk told him bluntly that Gould was in a tight place, and that all depended upon whether or not the government would hold its gold. Corbin replied that they need not have the least fear, and was given twenty-five thousand dollars to transmit to Mrs. Grant as "profit."

The president and General Porter were sojourning at Washington, Pennsylvania, at the time. Gould wanted further assurance and insisted that Corbin send a message to the president and get an answer. Gould furnished a confidential man, who journeyed to the town and presented Corbin's note to Grant. He read it and said, "All right." The contents were never made known, but on the strength of this cryptic reply, the game went on. The uneasiness, however, was not allayed, and Corbin was sought out again by Fisk. Corbin brought his wife, the president's sister, into the consultation. "I know there will be no gold sold by the government," she said. "I am quite positive there will be no gold sold. This is a lifetime chance for us. You need have no uneasiness whatever."

This did not relieve Fisk's uncertainties, however. He knew all the real gold in New York was in their hands. What they were now buying was the phantom gold, sold by the shorts. This could give

no trouble. The fear lay in the Treasury's coming
to the relief of the shorts. That Corbin was fool-
ing them, seemed possible to Fisk; Gould seems to
have been full of faith. Thursday morning, September twenty-third, after the evening interview,
they drove down-town together. "Old Corbin feels
nervous about some gold," said Gould. "He wants
one hundred thousand dollars. What do you think
about it?"

The astute Fisk thought that if he wanted it
for "parties in interest," he had better have it.
Gould agreed, and Fisk went to Smith, Gould,
Martin and Company and got the sum, giving it
to Gould, who said he would stop on the way home
that night and deliver it.

"Somehow or other," Fisk said in testifying
later, "when I was not with Corbin, I always felt
shaky about the old rascal. I had my suspicions
all the time, and yet, when he talked to me, I
thought he was as innocent and guileless as a baby.
But I kept my suspicions to myself."

He knew Gould was "in up to the handle," by
his habit of tearing up paper into small pieces
when mentally disturbed.

Friday morning, September twenty-fourth,
dawned a memorable day. Gold opened at one
hundred and forty-five, but no one offered to sell.
Gould and Fisk were calling the shorts, and these
could not make good. The wildest excitement followed. Bid after bid was shrieked in a vain effort

to meet the rise, but there was no relief. Gold rose point by point until it touched one hundred and sixty-two. Then a voice in the crowd said quietly, "One million dollars sold at one hundred and sixty-two." This was the top notch and stopping point.

With the country in an agony of panic a tornado of telegrams had blown in on Secretary Boutwell. He transmitted word of the situation to Grant, who was playing a quiet game of croquet with Horace Porter at Washington, Pennsylvania. He ordered the sale of five million dollars in government gold to relieve the stress. The remedy was instantly effective. Buying bids ceased. There was a terrific rush to sell, but no one bought. Soon the retreating figures reached one hundred and thirty-five. As a chronicler of the dreadful day observed: "The gigantic gold bubble had burst, and half Wall Street was involved in ruin."

Fisk bore the brunt with his usual effrontery. He neither settled nor enforced settlement. Gould disposed of his gold. How far Corbin profited has never been revealed. "Mr. and Mrs. Corbin deceived me," Fisk testified.

"What became of the gold carried for Mrs. Grant and the other members of the president's family?" he was asked.

"Oh, that went with the rest," was the adventurer's immortal reply, "to 'where the woodbine twineth.'"

The conclusion of his examination is of interest:

"Do you know whether any money was paid to Mrs. Grant?"

"I only know what that old thief Corbin told me. Corbin was paid twenty-five thousand dollars for Mrs. Grant in a check. I have already told you all about it."

"Do you know what the letter contained which Corbin sent to the president?"

"No. There's where we made a terrible blunder. There's where we were overreached. We ought to have found out the contents of the old villain's letter. It was that which sold us body, soul and breeches."

In this easy fashion was produced one of the most memorable monetary massacres in American history.

So far as President Grant was concerned, he was not unaware of the wiles of his venerable relation. Mrs. Grant wrote her sister-in-law, begging her to make her husband quit speculating. The twenty-five thousand dollars taken from Gould for Mrs. Grant was never sent her. When the canceled check came back, it was found that Corbin had used it to pay off a bank loan. He sold Grant "short," and only pretended to deliver.

Gould selected one Alfred Speyers to be his broker on the floor of the gold room. During the dusty day he bought sixty million dollars of phantom gold! It had been planned to use the Tenth

National Bank as a place of certification, but the inconvenient presence of a bank examiner spoiled the scheme. Gould, it appears, never lost his head, but "sitting pretty," so to speak, in his office in the Grand Opera House, played with events. He enjoined the Gold Exchange from taking any action on his deals, and with the breathing spell then afforded, was able, on October first, to begin making orderly adjustments, and came out nine million dollars ahead.

The crisis affected stocks as well, and but for some heroic work on the part of Commodore Vanderbilt, the panic would have extended to securities. He threw a million dollars into the whirlpool and stilled the waters. As it was, the Gold Exchange Bank was wrecked, and the Tenth National put into a receiver's hands.

Fisk's showy person and lavish ways caused him to be elected Colonel of the Ninth Regiment, N. G. S. N. Y. The Grand Opera House was near its armory, and the regiment, poor in numbers and weak in spirit, needed an angel, whom it found in Fisk. He was chosen by the officers at a meeting held on April 7, 1870, and soon made the regiment a center of interest. Its ranks filled up under the stimulus of a prize of five hundred dollars offered by the colonel to the company that should muster the most men on the first of July. On that date it numbered seven hundred in rank and file plus a brass band of one hundred pieces. Fisk was booming Long Branch, a celebrated New Jersey resort in ante-bellum days, and celebrated the swelling of ranks by taking the command on an excursion to the place on July twentieth. The stay lasted for a week, while the invasion of a friendly state was not resented, as Fisk paid all the bills. A grand ball ended the foray. The *Plymouth Rock* conveyed the command back to New York full of joy over the unusual picnic. Fisk was living the flashiest kind of a life, and his ways reflected on the regiment. It stood by him as one man, however, and kept up its festivities.

In February, 1871, a great ball was given at the Academy of Music, where Fisk and his staff paraded in all their glory. He was hailed as the Prince of Erie and continued to shock and amuse the community. His wife lived in Boston, and Fisk had always kept his legal residence in the Hub. It occurred to him that as a lesson in patriotism he would take the Ninth to the city and help celebrate the anniversary of the Battle of Bunker Hill, on June 17, 1871. For purposes of formality, he sent three of his officers bearing a note to Mayor William A. Gaston, to ask that the hospitality of the city be extended the regiment. The mayor did not deign to make reply, but referred the request to the common council, which rejected the suggestion with scorn, enhanced by the thought that it carried with it the need of an appropriation. Fisk learned the result from the press and applied to the governor for permission to invade the state at his own expense. This was granted, and Fisk so advised Gaston, with the comment that his discourtesy and that of the aldermen was a matter of indifference to both himself and the regiment. They were coming anyway under the higher warrant. The plan was to proceed by boat on the sixteenth, join the celebration on the seventeenth, have a dress parade on Sunday, and return that night. He asked permission to use the Common for the parade. This the mayor referred to the aldermen, who refused the desired permission.

The regiment reached Boston, was received by local militiamen and marched to Bunker Hill. As it was excluded from the Common, Fisk hired the Boston Theater, where the chaplain preached to the men, and the band gave a sacred concert led by Jules Levy, the celebrated cornetist. All returned in good humor, despite the official snub.

On July 12, 1871, came a trial of the colonel's metal. It did not shine much. There was a strong, vindictive feeling between the Irish Catholics of the city and the Orangemen, who asked permission to parade on that date in celebration of the anniversary of the Battle of the Boyne. Fearing trouble, Police Superintendent John J. Kelso refused a permit, but this was revoked by Governor John T. Hoffman, who ordered the police and the militia to protect the paraders. Accordingly, they set out at two P. M. on Eighth Avenue, headed by two hundred and fifty police and guarded further by the Seventh, the Twenty-second, Sixth, Eighty-fourth and Ninth Regiments.

The Orangemen, members of Gideon Lodge, numbered a bare hundred. The procession had moved several blocks and passed the Grand Opera House, when rioting began. Stones were thrown from neighboring roofs and between Twenty-seventh and Twenty-eighth Streets, a dense crowd blocked the avenue. The rioters stopped the march and became violent. Orders were given to clear the way, and not being obeyed, the soldiers fired, but Sergeants Henry E. Page and Samuel Wyatt of the Ninth Regiment had been killed, and Private Walter R. Pryor, mortally wounded. Volleys were fired until the crowd gave way, leaving forty-nine killed and eighty-seven wounded, of whom six died later. Eighteen soldiers and two policemen were injured.

Fisk was not with his regiment. His story was that after a midnight conference with Governor Hoffman and Mayor Hall, at which they discussed the question of stopping the Erie ferries in order to prevent Orangemen coming from New Jersey to add to the anticipated troubles, he had reached the armory at eight A. M., to expedite the muster of his men. Remaining until noon, when he received word that crowds were coming over on the Twenty-third Street ferry, he went to the

Grand Opera House to consult Gould about stopping the boats. Gould was not there, so he issued the order himself and left for the armory. The weather being warm and its wearer stout, he left his coat at the armory. The procession had started and he fell into rank with the Sixth Regiment, and worked along to the Ninth. Here he borrowed Major J. R. Hitchcock's sword and took command. The assault began on this regiment, which had been previously instructed not to fire unless assailed. The killing of the sergeants turned the soldiers loose. Fisk was engulfed in the crowd, knocked down and trampled upon. He could not rise, and some of the men carried him into a bakery, where the regimental surgeon found his ankle dislocated. It was jerked into place. The mob invaded the bakery, demanding vengeance, and, according to Fisk, he seized a heavy cane and fled, "jumping over at least five backyard fences," a considerable feat for one of his weight. He went through a house to Ninth Avenue, and coming out, saw some of the mob—"a hard-looking set," he put it—and ran through an open door in Twenty-seventh Street. He scaled more fences, and, entering a house, procured some old clothes in which he ventured out. He hailed a cab coming up Ninth Avenue. To his joy, he found the passenger inside was Jay Gould. Gould took him to the Hoffman House, where an excited crowd caused him to flee to Pavonia Ferry, whence an Erie tug bore him to Sandy Hook.

Here he took a train to Long Branch and, as he says, did not take off his disguise until he reached the Continental Hotel,—so ending what would appear to have been a rather inglorious day. He was not cashiered, however, and appeared in full luster at the head of the regiment when it formed part of the escort accorded the Russian Grand Duke Alexis when he visited New York on November 21, 1871. He even favored the royal guest with half an hour of breezy conversation.

He next diverted himself with trying to break into the Union Pacific Railway, offering to take a large block of stock on the basis of a small payment down. The proffer was declined. He then bought six shares, and posing as a wronged stockholder, demanded access to the company's books. This was denied, and one of his paid judges gave him an order which he executed with a gang of safe-breaking mechanics. Of course, he found nothing, but it made a big noise and scared the Union Pacific into moving its offices to Boston.

They were a strange pair—the large, florid Fisk with his showy ways, and the small, silent, shrinking Gould. It is related that once walking together near the Opera House, they were accosted by a beggar. Gould took out a roll of bills and began searching for one of small denomination. Fisk captured the roll and handed it to the mendicant with this rather pertinent remark, "Jay, never count charity."

Emboldened by the success of the Erie exploit,

THE DREADFUL DECADE

Fisk and Gould endeavored to apply the same tactics to the Albany and Susquehanna railroad. They secured nominal control through stock jobbing and a fake receivership, but failed to obtain physical possession of the property. Its offices and stock books were in Albany. The two financiers called to claim them. J. B. Van Valkenburgh, a stout Hollander, who was superintendent of the line, barred their entrance and when Fisk tried to break in, threw him down-stairs. Prompt legal measures then saved the road from being looted.

Moral conditions were at a low ebb in New York. Brazen beauties flaunted their charms in open houses and glittering equipages. One of these, Helen Josephine Mansfield, was a factor in Fisk's affairs. He maintained her in a gorgeously furnished home at 359 West Twenty-fourth Street, near the Opera House, where she kept a *salon* much frequented by politicians and men about town. She was a California girl, the wife of Frank Lawlor, a minor actor of the day, who had brought her to New York. Here they soon parted by the divorce route. Frequenting theatrical circles, she met the monarch of the Grand Opera House through Annie Wood, an actress. The conquest was easy. Fisk's own residence was near by, at 313 West Twenty-third Street, and a private telegraph wire ran from his office in the Grand Opera House to Miss Mansfield's boudoir.

FISK AND GOULD

In addition to his other enterprises, Fisk put Long Branch, New Jersey, on the map again. The place had lost its chief patronage when the rich southern planters ceased their visits with the coming of the war. He frequented the resort with Miss Mansfield, and brought a following. The young woman set the fashions for the Branch, which soon became the center of gay and fast summer life, though one hotel man sought damages for the loss of respectable patronage through Fisk's coming to his house. The woman served Fisk's purpose and led many a man into his trap. One of these chanced to be Edward Stiles Stokes, scion of a celebrated family that had piled up wealth as members of the metal-dealing firm of Phelps, Stokes and Company, now Phelps, Dodge and Company. His father, Edward H. Stokes, had retired to Philadelphia, where Edward was born. Handsome and attractive, he had married, but had not settled down. He became an active member of the Fisk-Gould coterie.

The discovery of oil in Pennsylvania had added fury to the stock gambling of the day. All sorts of oil and refining companies were floated. Stokes had already made and lost a fortune in oil, partly on the Exchange, and partly through the destruction by fire of an uninsured plant. He regained his financial feet, but needing transportation for his crude oil, he took Fisk into his company and so secured inside rates over the Erie to Hunter's

Point, at tidewater. The two were often together at the Mansfield mansion, where Fisk met his intimates, and this gave rise to the belief that Stokes and Fisk were rivals.

However this might be, Stokes was soon in the lead with the lady, who was much put out by Fisk's penchant for Mademoiselle Montaland, a performer imported from Paris, who displayed her charms liberally upon the stage of the Grand Opera House. In her pique, Miss Mansfield openly favored Stokes and became his aid in the contest that ensued with Fisk.

Perceiving the profitable prospects in the oil industry, Fisk began an effort to force Stokes out of the control of his company. The camel had got his head inside the tent and wanted room for his body. This Stokes resisted. He was treasurer of the corporation, and Fisk had him arrested, January 4, 1871, on a charge of embezzling fifty thousand dollars. Justice Joseph Dowling dismissed the case as one of malicious prosecution.

Fisk now reverted to his usual practise. He ousted Stokes as treasurer of the oil company and put armed men in charge of the refinery. Stokes soon regained possession. Fisk cut off the favorable rates. Stokes then sought to charter a pipeline from the oil fields to the sea to free himself from the clutches of the Erie. Fisk used his ownership of the New York Legislature to prevent this. His "pull" was too much for Stokes, who then threatened to expose the manner in which Fisk and Gould were swindling stockholders of the road by granting special rates to concerns into which they had forced entrance, as in his own case.

Fisk and Gould secured an injunction from Judge Calvin E. Pratt, of Brooklyn, which stopped the publication of letters and documents that would have proved his case. Peter B. Sweeny was made custodian of the papers, while Clarence Seward, son of William H. Seward, was selected as arbitrator in the dispute over Stokes' claims. He decided against him on the important issues, but awarded ten thousand dollars damages to Stokes for the malicious prosecution.

All these things gave Gould great anxiety. Fisk was now vice-president of the Erie, and Gould became sensible that the relationship was doing the road no good. He therefore very timidly asked Fisk to resign. The Prince of Erie gave way to tears, but told Gould he would sign whatever was written, and Gould penned the note that ended his connection with the road.

The war with Stokes went on. Fisk now attempted to have Stokes indicted for extortion. In the course of the proceedings he caused to be published an affidavit made by Richard E. King, an ex-butler in the Mansfield entourage, alleging a blackmailing conspiracy between Stokes and the Mansfield woman. This, Miss Mansfield made the occasion for a suit for criminal libel against

Fisk. It had a hearing before Justice Bixby in the Yorkville Police Court on November 25, 1871, at which Fisk was defended by Charles S. Spencer and ex-Judge William A. Beach, while John McKeon and the gallant John R. Fellows, not long from the ranks of the Confederacy, represented the lady, who was attended to court by Edward S. Stokes and her cousin, Mrs. Williams.

An enthusiastic reporter has left this glimpse of Josephine Mansfield on the occasion: "Miss Mansfield looked extraordinarily handsome. Imagine a woman young and vivid, with full, dashing figure, yet not gross, with deep, large, almond-shaped black eyes, luxuriant purple-black hair worn in massive coils, tempting mouth, lips not too pronounced and yet not insipid, magnificent teeth, clear pearl and pink complexion, oval face and nose not *retroussé* and yet not straight, with a quiet ladylike walk and action, sweet soft voice and winning smile. Dress such a woman in a dark silk, flounced with deep Valenciennes, a flowing silk jacket beautifully embroidered with white braid, and a plain gold cross to set off the exquisite contour of her neck, and a dark green Tyrolese hat falling partly over her fair forehead, surmounted by a waving ostrich feather, and you have this Helen Josephine Mansifeld as she appeared yesterday."

She gave her age as twenty-four and took excellent care of herself on the stand—so good, in fact, that Fisk fled before her smiles. The spectators cheered her at adjournment, and the reporter who wrote an engaging account of the hearing for the *World,* indulged, at the conclusion of his vivacious recital, in a bit of prophecy the outcome of which he could hardly have anticipated. He said: "As Miss Mansfield, accompanied by her cousin, Mrs. Williams, and Mr. Stokes withdrew, she was loudly cheered. Two weeks hence the curtain will ring upon the tragical comedy of the loves of the modern Trojan warrior and the fairest of Helens."

The case did not come up in two weeks, as adjourned, but went over until Saturday, January 6, 1872. Stokes and Miss Mansfield attended and testified against Fisk in the matter of the alleged libel. Fisk did not appear. The lady made liberal use of tears under the cutting queries of Mr. Beach. Stokes denied that any of his relations with Miss Mansfield were improper, or that he had ever threatened to ruin Fisk. The case was then put over for another week. There was no hint of an impending tragedy.

According to his own account, Stokes went down-town from the court to ask his lawyer about the wisdom of taking a trip to Providence while under the possible indictment. He was told to go. His next move was to take a cab and pay a call at the Mansfield mansion. Finding the blinds drawn he ordered the driver to go down to the corner of Fourth Street and Broadway. Here he went into a sporting resort kept by Dodge and Chamberlain, where he met a horse dealer named Smith, with whom he had some dealings, and after a conference, walked down Broadway with a friend, George W. Bailey, until opposite the Grand Central Hotel, then the most splendid hostelry in town.

He was a debonair lady-killer of thirty, and as he looked across to the hotel, a woman smiled at him from a parlor window on the third story. He thought, he afterward said, she was some one he had met at Saratoga, crossed the street, went upstairs to the parlor and found he was mistaken. He sauntered slowly along the corridor and was descending the private staircase, when by some strange will of fate, James Fisk, Jr., garbed in a silk hat and the heavy military cloak he affected, came up. What happened, only Stokes could tell. He claimed that Fisk drew a weapon, and that he, Stokes, called out: "Don't shoot." He then fired two shots himself from a four-chamber revolver. Two took effect, one in Fisk's abdomen, the other in a leg.

Fisk fell on the stairs, and Stokes, walking toward the street, informed Charles G. Hill, the only person he met, that a man had been shot. He then proceeded to the office and asked the clerk to call a doctor. A crowd had now collected, and several laid hands on Stokes. He told them he did

not intend to escape and gave himself up to the
first policeman who came in. The officer led him
to where Fisk was lying on a sofa. Fisk identified Stokes, who was taken into custody by Police Captain Thomas F. Byrnes, later the famous
inspector, duly held and indicted for murder.
At the preliminary hearing, Miss Minnie J. Ben-
ton, a guest at the hotel, said she had picked up an
ivory-handled pistol. The woman was sent to the
House of Detention, but neither she nor the pistol
was present at the trial.

Fisk died at ten forty-five on Sunday, January
7, 1872. The city boiled with excitement. Some
hot-heads in the Ninth Regiment proposed to
storm the Tombs and lynch the killer. Fisk's body
lay in gorgeous state in the Grand Opera House
in a rosewood coffin graced with solid gold bars.
Jay Gould and William M. Tweed were chief
mourners, standing beside the coffin and weeping
freely. Tweed, under bail at the time, was quoted
as saying that Fisk was "a man of broad soul and
kindly heart; in his business transactions he was
governed by principles which seemed peculiar,
without being insincere, and were, perhaps, apparently dishonest, without being otherwise than enterprising." He knew, he said, that Fisk had "done
more good turns for worthy but embarrassed men
than all the clergymen in New York."

Many leading citizens attended the services.
The Ninth Regiment followed the hearse to

the depot, whence the casket was taken to Brattleboro for interment. His will made his wife, Lucy D. Fisk, and his former partner, Eben D. Jordan, its executors. All the ill-gotten property, save one hundred thousand dollars willed to his sister and several other small legacies, went to his widow. Her maiden name was Lucy D. Moore. She had met Fisk while in school at Brattleboro and married him at Ashland, Massachusetts, in 1855. She was an orphan. There were no children. He kept her in stylish surroundings in Boston, while he lived apart.

The trial was a *cause célèbre*. It was brought out that Fisk had gone to the hotel to call on Mrs. Edward C. Morse, an acquaintance, and Stokes, who took the stand, swore the meeting was entirely one of chance. He pleaded self-defense when the case came up before Judge Ingraham. The trial resulted in a verdict of murder in the first degree. On the Fisk side, it was urged that the millions of the Stokes family were enlisted to save a scion from the gallows; on the other, that corrupt financiers and Tammany were bent upon his death. The second trial gave a verdict of manslaughter, under which he received a four-year sentence and went to Sing Sing. Here he led an easy life, keeping a fine pair of horses at a local livery-stable and being allowed to drive them about after dark. His privileges were a scandal. Released, he built over the Hoffman House at Broadway and

Twenty-sixth Street, and remained its landlord until his death. The up-state Democrats made it their headquarters. Its chief attraction was a beautiful barroom adorned with fine paintings, the best of which was Bouguereau's *Nymphs and Satyr*—the young women being extremely *decolletée*. He lived until November 2, 1901.

Fisk had a fancy for singing birds. He kept several hundred in his rooms and on board the steamers. The canaries dwelt in gilt cages and each had a pet name given by their owner. These were sold at auction after his death and brought high prices from the curious.

Although Jay Gould wept beside James Fisk's bier, the move to make him resign was the result of a deep-laid plan to raise the status of the Erie by bringing men of standing into its affairs. William Butler Duncan suggested the plan, which Gould accepted, but did not mention to Fisk. His death cleared the way to respectability, could Gould have followed it. Gould had split with James McHenry, who controlled the Atlantic and Great Western, and threw the Atlantic and Great Western into a receivership, Gould and W. A. O'Doherty becoming the receivers. Through this it was manipulated so that the line was leased to the Erie. Later he broke the lease, and McHenry, in revenge, organized the Erie's foreign shareholders against Gould, who, in trying to defend himself, fell victim to an extraordinary swindler calling himself Lord Gordon Gordon, Earl of Aberdeen, and who pretended to control a big block of the foreign stock. The fellow had fallen in with Mrs. William Belden, wife of Fisk's partner at Minneapolis, in the fall of 1871, and evidently gained full knowledge of Erie affairs from the lady. He had been making a social stir in Minneapolis, and, coming to New York, took rooms at the Metropolitan Hotel, then managed by Richard M. Tweed, son of the boss, and made New York take notice. He represented that he controlled sixty thousand shares of Erie held in England, and got well in with Commodore Vanderbilt, Belden, Horace Greeley and Colonel Thomas A. Scott, of the Pennsylvania. By clever posing, he convinced Belden that he was the real thing and was urged to get together with Gould. He held off, but interested Scott, who advised Gould to call on the chilly aristocrat. March 8, 1872, Scott telegraphed Gould an introduction, armed with which he called on Gordon Gordon, at the Metropolitan.

There Gordon actually convinced that master of guile that he held the sixty thousand shares in the names of others, and had effected a combination to oust him. Horace Greeley was present at the interview. Gordon laid down conditions that to save himself Gould should cease opposition to the repeal, then pending at Albany, of a Classification Act which had enabled the Erie to squeeze shippers; that he should settle all litigation; and as an evidence of good faith, that he should give Gordon Gordon his resignation to be held for fulfillment of his promises. Gordon also asserted that he had arranged for the resignation of the directors, whom he would replace as soon as fifty million dollars in stock certificates reached him from London. Incidentally, he said he had spent one million dollars investigating Erie and thought he ought to get five hundred thousand dollars back.

This was the stake the scamp was playing for. Amazing as it may seem, Gould assented and actually gave him cash and securities to that amount. The cash amounted to two hundred thousand dollars and was in Gordon's hands from March 9 to March 23, 1872. He could have safely decamped, but did not. Some securities, to a small amount, he sent for sale to a broker in Philadelphia. The rest he kept in his rooms at the Metropolitan. On March twenty-third, Gould at last "smelled a rat" and confided his suspicions to William M. Tweed. Tweed sent for his friend, Judge Edward J. Shandley, and John J. Kelso, Superintendent of Police. In company with William Belden, they went to the Metropolitan. Notice was served on Gordon to give up. He did, to the astonishment of all hands. Subsequently Gordon was ordered arrested on charges of embezzling the stock sent to Philadelphia.

Gordon brought a counter-suit against Gould for the balance of the five hundred thousand dollars returned. The hearing was down for September 20, 1872. Before the day, Gordon disappeared. He subsequently turned up in Manitoba. As he had "stuck" his bondsmen thirty-seven thousand dollars, they tried to get him back to New York. Two detectives who followed him were arrested and jailed on the charge of attempted kidnapping. Later, two more took him in custody on August 1, 1874. Their papers were bogus, but Gordon agreed to go with them, on an alleged charge of embezzlement in England and Scotland. Excusing himself for a moment, he blew out his brains in the next room. It turned out that he had been guilty of swindles in England and Scotland. Gould got back the securities from the Philadelphia brokers. So endeth the extraordinary tale.

Meanwhile, McHenry, in London, had continued his efforts and had interested General Daniel E. Sickles, who engaged to tackle Gould. By March, 1872, the forces were aligned. Gould was offered five hundred thousand dollars to part with control. This he refused. Force followed. The board met Monday, March 11, 1872. Gould, through Thomas G. Shearman, counsel for the Erie, had procured an injunction from Judge Ingraham, claiming conspiracy. Gould was not present, but Shearman was backed by Superintendent Kelso and a score of police. The directors declined to obey the injunction or to be intimidated by the police. General John A. Dix was elected a director in Fisk's place, and a number of resignations made way for the election of General George B. McClellan, S. L. M. Barlow, William R. Travers, William Watts Sherman, Colonel Henry G. Stebbins, General A. S. Diven, Charles Drake and Charles Day. General Dix was elected president. Gould fortified himself in the president's office. Vice-President O. H. R. Archer defied his orders and tore down his proclamations. He held on until the morning of March twelfth, when, finding himself abandoned by all the officers of the company, he made his last play. This was to call a new meeting, to which his opponents agreed. Then he resigned, and the program went through as before. The new board hired T. G. Shearman as counsel. March fifteenth, Gould retired from the directorate. Sickles had said to him: "If you resign, Erie will go up fifteen points. You can make a million dollars."

It went up twenty points, and Gould, on the long side for once, paid himself well for his humiliation and retirement. This was his last appearance in Erie, out of which he had made himself rich and many others poor, besides imposing on the road and its territory a burden of obligations that have cramped both for more than fifty years. Incidentally he was forced to hand back some six million dollars in Erie shares which belonged to the company, but which, for purposes of control, he treated as his own.

THE DREADFUL DECADE

In November, 1872, Gould engineered a neat corner in Chicago and Northwestern stock, pinching Uncle Daniel Drew, who ⸱ vily short. The result was Gould's arr November twenty-second, on a civil action to ⸱ over nine million dollars alleged to have been abstracted by him during his rule of Erie as president and treasurer. He gave bail in one million dollars, Augustus Schell and Horace E. Clark becoming his sureties, and went back to the office of Smith, Gould, Martin and Company, to attend to Uncle Daniel. On November twenty-first the stock had started up at eighty-three and skied to two hundred before two days, with large transactions.

Drew made his headquarters at 51 Exchange Place, in a private office, but was represented by his brokerage concern, Kenyon, Cox and Company. Gould maintained his corner and forced settlements. Kenyon, Cox and Company were sold out under the rule, being in default on their contracts.

The *World* described Daniel Drew at the moment of the Northwestern excitement in this fashion: "Daniel showed himself to the vulgar outsiders very seldom, and then, with his ruffled, aged silk hat upon the back part of his head, his pants, like Mr. Greeley's, half-way up to his knees, held up by the strap of his bootlegs, and a cigar in his mouth, would lean over the indicator (ticker), blow a clear space through the cloud of smoke, and

JAY GOULD

see for himself what the genuine quotations of Northwestern were."

Gould made his headquarters in the office of Osborn and Chapin and explained his troubles thus: "The matter is very simple. Drew, Smith and the rest of them were short of stock, and, as a desperate resort, they watched their time and arranged matters so as to have me arrested just at the moment they expected to be able to create a panic in the street—not to be seriously prosecuted in the courts." Absence from Erie did not curtail his ambitions. Other roads, notably the Wabash and Missouri Pacific came under his evil ken, until at the time of his decease he controlled twenty-two thousand miles of railway, the elevated system in New York City and the Western Union telegraph, building a fortune of seventy-five million dollars to demoralize his family and become a sordid long-drawn-out scandal and litigation, while he all his lifetime was shunned, hated and despised and went about always under guard for fear of personal assaults which were more than once attempted.

Gould died in New York City, December 2, 1892, when but fifty-six. Fisk was thirty-seven when Stokes' pistol shot put an end to his career.

CHAPTER III

CREDIT MOBILIER

Corruption in the Construction of the Union Pacific Railroad—
Oakes Ames and His Fellow Financiers—The Great Scandal—Panic
of 1873—Failure of Jay Cooke and Company—Countrywide
Consequences—Greenback Movement.

THE Credit Mobilier, which bred so much scandal in the construction of the Union Pacific railroad, built to link the Atlantic with the Pacific, was formed on the lines of the Credit Mobilier of France, a joint stock corporation established in Paris, November 18, 1852, for the general purpose of financing corporations. The idea was brought to the United States by George Francis Train, founder of Omaha and one of the active promoters of the Union Pacific, although his name does not appear in the records. His disturbed mental state took him out of the transactions involved before they became subjects for investigation.

The American imitation had its inception in Pennsylvania, where, in 1859, there was incorporated the Pennsylvania Fiscal Company by Samuel J. Reeves, Ellis Lewis, Garrick Mallory, Duff Green, David R. Porter, Jacob Ziegler, Charles M. Hall, H. R. Kneass, Robert J. Ross, William T. Dougherty, Isaac Hugus, C. M. Reed, William

CREDIT MOBILIER

Workman, Asa Packer, Jesse Lazear, C. S. Kauffman, C. L. Ward and Henry M. Fuller, It was given powers under the charter to buy, sell, contract, lease, mortgage or convey, the primary purpose being the purchase and sale of railway securities, or to advance money to such enterprises "on such terms as might be agreed upon." In short, a very wide-open set of privileges and small responsibilities were thus acquired. The war checked any operations, and no election of officers was held until May 29, 1863, when Jacob Ziegler became president, Oliver Barnes, secretary, and Charles M. Hall, treasurer. The Union Pacific was being pressed as a measure of national safety, and on March 3, 1864, the Pennsylvania Fiscal Company's charter was bought by Thomas C. Durant, Vice-President of the Union Pacific. On March twenty-sixth the corporate name of the concern was changed to "The Credit Mobilier of America," by act of the Pennsylvania Legislature, with none of its privileges curtailed. One of these was the right to open an agency in New York, under which it promptly moved all its operations to the Metropolis, adding thereto a Railway Bureau. Seven managers were provided in making the change, and these at once took up the task of constructing the Union Pacific. That company had issued two million, one hundred and eighty thousand dollars' worth of stock, upon which the subscribers had only paid in ten per cent.—or two

hundred and eighteen thousand dollars. This the
Credit Mobilier refunded and took over the holdings. The stock had a par value of one thousand
dollars per share. Congress passed an act cancel-
ing this stock and permitting a new issue on a one-
hundred-dollar per share basis, which was made to
the stockholders in the Credit Mobilier. Thus the
contracting corporation became the owner of the
road as well as its constructor, with all the advantages of the Pennsylvania Charter intact.

The Union Pacific had been incorporated in
1862 by an act of Congress which carried with it
land grants for every mile to be built, plus government bonds. The only limit to be observed by
the corporation was to keep the stock at one hundred million dollars, with the condition that none
should be sold for less than one hundred dollars
per share. In spite of the fat inducements, the
war kept capital out of investments, and in July,
1864, the government doubled the grants of land
and permitted the issuing of bonds, which were
to be a first mortgage, the government taking a
second mortgage for its own security. The company had in the meantime spent about six hundred
thousand dollars in construction, or nearly four
hundred thousand dollars more than the two hundred and eighteen thousand dollars paid in
assessments on the stock.

The new arrangements permitted more energy.
August 8, 1864, H. M. Hoxie contracted to build

one hundred miles west from Omaha for fifty thousand dollars a mile and to take bonds in payment. He gave up, after a slight attempt, and on March 15, 1865, assigned his agreement to the Credit Mobilier. Hoxie, in return for this relief, promised to take and pay for five hundred thousand dollars' worth of stock in the road. This was accepted by John A. Dix, C. S. Bushnell and George T. M. Davis, a special committee appointed to attend to the transaction. Before cancellation, Hoxie's contract was extended to two hundred and forty-seven miles, and this increased obligation went to the Credit Mobilier with the approval of the committee which represented the railroad—the right hand washing the left. Under this dubious arrangement the Credit Mobilier completed the Hoxie contract at a cost of $7,806,183.33, and received in securities, government and railway, $12,974,416.24—a very tidy profit for taking no risk at all!

Thomas C. Durant, on behalf of the Union Pacific, now contracted with one Boomer to build one hundred and fifty-three miles of road for nineteen thousand, five hundred and, for varying sections, twenty thousand dollars per mile. The company failed to ratify the contract, though Boomer built fifty-eight miles, but instead extended the assigned Hoxie contract over the completed track and put the Credit Mobilier in a position to exact a profit approximating one million, three hundred and forty-five thousand dollars, the road having been accepted by the government and the land warrants and bonds being handed over therefor. The effort to exact fifty thousand dollars a mile, for what, with stations and all extras (according to Mr. Durant), cost but twenty-seven thousand, five hundred dollars, was thwarted by him when he succeeded in blocking the resolution covering the transaction January 5, 1867. Durant had been dropped from the board of the Credit Mobilier and was temporarily firm in his purpose to stop the fleecing.

A new move to circumvent Durant was now made in awarding a contract for two hundred and sixty-seven miles at fifty thousand dollars a mile, to J. M. S. Williams, Williams having agreed to assign the same to the Credit Mobilier. It reacted to cover the mileage built and paid for by the railroad under the Boomer agreement. Durant again intervened and brought matters to a standstill until Oakes Ames came upon the scene and with him the celebrated scandal attached to Credit Mobilier. Ames contracted on August 16, 1867, to complete six hundred and sixty-seven miles on the following terms: One hundred miles at forty-two thousand dollars per mile; one hundred and sixty-seven miles at forty-five thousand dollars per mile; one hundred miles at ninety-six thousand dollars per mile; one hundred miles at eighty thousand dollars per mile; one hundred miles at ninety thousand dollars

CREDIT MOBILIER

per mile; one hundred miles at ninety-six thousand
dollars per mile. Ames was only a cloak to hide
the hoofs and horns of the pillagers in the Credit
Mobilier, of whom he was one, as evidenced by the
fact that sixty days later he had assigned this rich
undertaking to the concern. Durant, Oliver
Ames, brother of Oakes, L. S. Bushnell and
Springer Harbaugh signed on behalf of the Union
Pacific. The assignment was made on October
15, 1867. The ratifiers were Thomas C. Durant,
who had been pacified; Oliver Ames, of North
Easton, Massachusetts, the seat of the Ames
family shovel industries, John B. Alley, of Lynn,
Massachusetts, Sidney Dillon, of New York, Cornelius S. Bushnell, of New Haven; Henry S.
McComb, of Washington, Delaware, and Benjamin E. Bates, of Boston. Sidney Dillon headed the
Credit Mobilier. The seven men named accepted
the assignment as trustees. Assent in writing of
the stockholders of the road was also given.

Work was now expedited with such vigor that
on December 12, 1867, Credit Mobilier was able
to declare a dividend consisting of $2,244,000 in
Union Pacific bonds and an equal amount of its
stock. The sale of government bonds had furnished the working capital. Apologists point out
that the bonds were marketable at eighty and the
stock at thirty, so the dividend was worth only
$2,580,600!

The remaining one hundred and twenty-five

miles of road were built under what was called the "Davis" contract, on the same terms as the Ames contract, though the cost of pushing the line through the Rockies was vastly below the price per mile allowed. In the end, the road was six million dollars in debt, with a colossal outstanding capitalization in stocks and bonds, and an amiable government carrying the bag. The chief benefit of the line befell the Mormons of Utah and the adventurers who now proceeded recklessly to slaughter the buffalo and promote expensive Indian wars. Tabulated, the account ran:

Cost to the Railroad Company

Hoxie contract	$12,974,416.24
Ames contract	57,140,102.94
Davis contract	23,431,768.10

Total cost	$93,546,287.28

Cost to the Contractors

Hoxie contract	$ 7,806,183.33	
Ames contract	27,285,141.99	
Davis contract	15,629,633.62	50,720,958.94

Profits at par values	$42,825,328.34

The railroad costs are all set at par, not at the market rates, but they represent the extravagant load piled on the line. Condensed to cash, however, at quotations of the time, the loot netted $23,374,914.81 to the profit of Credit Mobilier.

CREDIT MOBILIER

To produce this, the United States had lent its credit to the extent of $27,236,512, and the railroad had bonded itself for $27,213,000, or had assumed a grand total in obligations of $54,449,512. Yet in its finality the Credit Mobilier claimed to have had a net profit of but $8,141,903.70. Such was the wastage in capital and shrinkage in security values by reason of the way they were disposed of. This, however, did not serve to lighten the burden carried by the road.

During the long period of construction, Oakes Ames was an influential member of Congress and represented a Massachusetts district when the famous scandal broke. The exposé was due to the action of Henry S. McComb to enforce the delivery to himself of two hundred fifty shares of Credit Mobilier stock for which he had subscribed in 1866, on behalf of H. G. Fant, a Washington broker, who failed to honor a draft for twenty-five thousand dollars drawn in payment. This draft was protested and in due season returned to McComb. By what process other than blackmail McComb could claim any right to the shares, is not plain. Indeed, his motive was evident, but Ames and his associates declined to be held up. The result was a suit which brought to light sundry letters written by Ames to McComb, showing the distribution of stock among statesmen in order to procure friends for his great enterprise.

This suit dragged along for several years,

until 1872, when Judge Jeremiah S. Black, who was McComb's counsel, advised John B. Alley that the suit had better be settled, as McComb possessed evidence of bribery. Alley laughed at the idea, and when Black offered to compromise for one hundred thousand dollars, he was defied by Mr. Ames and his associates. Black was an intimate friend of Charles A. Dana, editor of the *New York Sun,* and upon this refusal, gave him the Oakes Ames letters. They were duly printed and made it plain that Ames had distributed some stock by sale to fellow congressmen. That he did it from what could be called corrupt motives was not in his own conscience to believe. He was only "taking care of friends,"—who might be useful, though there was no evidence adduced to show that they ever were.

The exposure, coming in a campaign year, raised a mighty stir, shattering the reputation of Schuyler Colfax, the vice-president, driving Ames from public life with a broken spirit, besmirching a number of congressmen who did not tell the truth, and doing such harm to the Republican party as would have cost it the election, had any other than Horace Greeley been selected to oppose Grant for his second term.

The first letter read:

Washington, January 25, 1868.
H. S. McComb, Esq.,
    Dear Sir: Yours of the twenty-third is at

hand, in which you say Senators Bayard and Fowler have written you in relation to their stock. I have spoken to Fowler, but not to Bayard; I have never been introduced to Bayard, but will see him soon. You say I must not put too much in one locality. I have assigned as far as I have gone to: four from Massachusetts, one from New Hampshire, one Delaware, one Tennessee, one Ohio, two Pennsylvania, one Indiana, one Maine, and I have three to place, which I shall place where they will do most good to us. I am here on the spot, and can better judge where they should go. I think after this dividend is paid, we should make our capital four million, and distribute the new stock where it will protect us—let them have the stock at par, and profits made in the future; the fifty per cent. increase on the old stock, I want for distribution here, and soon. Alley is opposed to the division of the bonds; says we will need them, &c., &c. I should think we ought to be able to spare them, with Alley and Cisco on the finance committee; we used to be able to borrow when we had no credit and debts pressing. We are now out of debt and in good credit—what say you about the bond dividend? A part of the purchasers here are poor and want their bonds to sell to enable them to meet their payment on the stock in the Credit Mobilier. I have told them what they would get as dividend, and they expect, I think, the bonds the parties receive as the eighty per cent. dividend; we better give them the bonds—it will not amount to anything with us. Some of the large holders will not care whether they have the bonds or certificates, or they will lend their bonds to the company as they have done before, or lend them money.

Quigley has been here, and we have got that one-tenth that was Underwood's. I have taken half, Quigley one-fourth, and you one-fourth. J. Carter wants a part of it; at some future day we will surrender a part to him.

Yours truly,
OAKES AMES.

This is the text of the second missive:

Washington, January 30, 1868.
H. S. McComb,

Dear Sir: Yours of the twenty-eighth is at hand, enclosing a letter from, or rather to, Mr. King. I don't fear any investigation here. What some of Durant's friends may do in New York courts can't be counted upon with any certainty. You do not understand, by your letter, what I have done, and am to do with my sales of stock. You say none to New York. I have placed some with New York, or have agreed to. You must remember it was nearly all placed, as you saw on the list in New York, and there were but six or eight thousand for me to place. I could not give all the world all they might want out of that. You would not want me to offer less than one thousand to any one. We allow Durant to place fifty-eight thousand to some three or four of his friends, or keep it himself.

I have used this where it will produce most good to us, I think. In view of King's letter, and Washington's move here, I go in for making our bond dividend in full. We can do it with perfect safety. I understand the opposition to it comes from Alley; he is on the finance com'ee and can raise money easy if we come short, which I don't believe we shall; and if we do, we can loan our bonds to the company, or loan them the money we got from the bonds. The contract calls for the division, and I say, have it. When shall I see you in Washington?   Yours truly,

OAKES AMES.

A third note completed the revelation:

Washington, February 22, 1868.
H. S. McComb, Esq.,
    Dear Sir: Yours of the twenty-first is at hand; am glad to hear that you are getting along so well with Mr. West, and hope you will bring it out all satisfactory, so that it will be so rich that we can not help going into it. I return you the paper by mail that you ask for. You ask me if I will sell some of my Union Pacific Railroad stock. I will sell some of it at par, Credit Mobilier of America. I don't care to sell. I hear that Mr. Bates offered his at three hundred dollars, but I don't want Bates to sell out. I think Grimes may sell a part of his at three hundred fifty dollars. I want that fourteen thousand dollars increase of the Credit Mobilier to sell here. We want more friends in this Congress, and if a man will look into the law (and it is difficult for them to do it unless they have an interest to do so), he can not help being convinced that we should not be interfered with. Hope to see you here or at New York the eleventh.   Yours truly,

OAKES AMES.

Congress convened in December, 1872. As a result of the *Sun's* publication, on motion of James G. Blaine, who left the speaker's chair to

[107]

make it, an investigation committee was appointed, headed by Congressman Luke P. Poland, of Vermont. His associates were Nathaniel P. Banks, of Massachusetts, James B. Beck, of Kentucky, William E. Niblack, of Indiana and George W. McCrary, of Iowa. Grant had been reelected, with Henry Wilson, of Massachusetts, as vice-president, replacing the unlucky Colfax. The committee held secret sessions for a time, but was soon forced into the open. Meantime, their actions caused the appointment on January 6, 1873, of another committee, comprising J. M. Wilson, of Indiana, Samuel Shellabarger, of Ohio, George F. Hoar, of Massachusetts, Thomas Swann, of Maryland, and General Henry W. Slocum, of New York, "to inquire whether or not any person connected with the reorganization or association commonly known as the 'Credit Mobilier,' now holds any of the bonds of the Union Pacific Railroad Company, for the payment of which, or the interest thereon, the United States is in any way liable; and whether or not, such holders, if any, or their assignees, of such bonds, are holders in good faith, and for value, or procured the same illegally or by fraud, and whether or not the United States may properly refuse to pay interest thereon, or the principal thereof, which the same shall become due, and whether or not any relinquishment of first mortgage lien that may theretofore have been made by the United States with reference to the bonds of said Railroad Company may be set aside, and to inquire into the character and purpose of such organization, and what officers of the United States or members of Congress have at any time been connected therewith, what connection it had with the contracts for the construction of said Union Pacific Railroad Company, and to report the facts to this House, together with such bill as may be necessary to protect the interests of the United States on account of any of the bonds of the class herein before referred to; and said committee is authorized to send for persons and papers, and to report any time."

The Poland Committee reported on February eighteenth, and the Wilson Committee on the nineteenth. The latter recommended an act to authorize a suit on behalf of the government to recover funds unlawfully sequestered in building the road. This was brought by the attorney-general before the Circuit Court in Connecticut. The government was defeated, the court holding:

This bill exhibits no right to relief on the part of the United States founded on the charter contract. The company has constructed its road to completion, keeps it in running order and carries for the government all that is required of it. It owes the government nothing that is due, and the government has the security which by law it provided. Nor does the bill show anything which authorizes the United States, as the depository of a trust, public or private, to sustain the suit.

This was affirmed by the United States Supreme Court.

The Poland report, dealing with the morals of Congress and Oakes Ames, gave absolution to many. John A. Logan had subscribed for ten shares but had not paid for them. Ames cared for them out of a dividend which left Logan a cash balance of three hundred twenty-nine dollars, which he took. This was in June, 1868. Not liking the aspect of the trade, he returned the money in July, and so was clear of it. Henry Wilson, then vice-president, had subscribed for twenty shares in 1867, on account of his wife. She paid two thousand dollars down, with an underwriting by Ames. Mr. Wilson returned his dividends, and Ames bought back the stock for the price paid. Wilson comforted his wife by giving her eight hundred fourteen dollars, which she might have retained as a dividend. This cleared him. James G. Blaine was asked to take ten shares by Ames, but declined, and was in no way concerned in the matter. Henry L. Dawes, afterward senator from Massachusetts, had owned ten shares bought in 1867. Hearing of the McComb suit in 1868, he gave back all he had received in the way of dividends, but accepted ten per cent. on the money for the time it had been invested. His hands were called clean. G. W. Scofield, of Pennsylvania, took ten shares, but on receiving a dividend of eighty per cent. in bonds and sixty per cent. in cash, felt it was too rich to hold and turned it all back. Ames rescinded the sale.

John A. Bingham, of Ohio, a Republican war-horse, bought twenty shares and held them until 1872, when he "cleaned up" *in toto,* receiving all dividends, etc. William D. (Pig Iron) Kelley, of Pennsylvania, bought, but did not pay for, ten shares. Ames carried them, paying for the stock out of the dividends and giving Kelley a profit of three hundred twenty-nine dollars, which he took. The same sort of transaction was found to have taken place with James A. Garfield, of Ohio. Garfield denied it, but the proof was plain. He said no more about it. B. F. Boyer, of Philadelphia, and his wife held one hundred shares. He had paid for them and denied that he had ever done any favor in return, asserting that it was a legitimate transaction, concerning which his only regret was that he had not bought more.

James Brooks, a Democratic congressman from New York, born in Portland, Maine, came out of the inquiry with blackened hands. He had taken one hundred shares, after making a demand for two hundred. As a government director of the Union Pacific, it was unlawful for him to possess any, so it was held in the name of his son-in-law, Charles H. Neilson. He paid ten thousand dollars for the shares, and received back twenty thousand dollars in Union Pacific stock and five thousand dollars cash. He demanded and received fifty shares more of Credit Mobilier, to which he had no moral or legal right. William B. Allison, of Iowa, was in the same class as Kelley and Garfield, paying no money down on ten shares. Ames credited him with dividends for the payment, and he held on. In 1868, he received six hundred dollars more. He returned the stock to Ames after the inquiry began, on the suggestion that he would take it back when the storm blew over. The committee did not reveal his turpitude. James W. Patterson, Senator from New Hampshire, had thirty shares and all the profits in his pockets. He equivocated. Vice-President Colfax was not named in the report, but he made a statement to the committee admitting that he had dealt with Ames to the extent of twenty shares, on which he paid five hundred dollars. He declared he had never got this back or received any dividends. Ames' testimony showed he had carried the stock and paid for it with dividends, less the amount given him by Colfax. He had paid him one dividend of one thousand two hundred dollars. This Colfax denied ever receiving. It was proved that he had taken the money.

The committee recommended that Senator Patterson be expelled. His term expired before any action could be taken. All the congressmen were absolved from corrupt intent but two, concerning whom the committee presented the following resolutions:

1. *Whereas,* Mr. Oakes Ames, a Representa-

tive in this House, from the State of Massachusetts, has been guilty of selling to members of Congress shares of stock in the Credit Mobilier of America, for prices much below the true value of such stock, with intent thereby to influence the votes and decisions of such members in matters to be brought before Congress for action: Therefore,

Resolved, That Mr. Oakes Ames be, and he is hereby, expelled from his seat as a member of this House.

2. *Whereas,* Mr. James Brooks, a Representative in this House from the State of New York, did procure the Credit Mobilier Company to issue and deliver to Charles H. Neilson, for the use and benefit of said Brooks, fifty shares of the stock of said company, at a price much below its real value, well knowing that the same was so issued and delivered with intent to influence the votes and decisions of said Brooks as a member of the House in matters to be brought before Congress for action, and also to influence the action of said Brooks as a government director in the Union Pacific Railroad Company: Therefore,

Resolved, That Mr. James Brooks be, and he is hereby, expelled from his seat as a member in this House.

Concerning Ames the report averred:

The members of Congress with whom he dealt were generally those who had been friendly and favorable to a Pacific Railroad, and Mr. Ames did not fear, or expect to find them favorable to movements hostile to it; but he desired to stimulate their

activity and watchfulness in opposition to any unfavorable action by giving them a personal interest
in the success of the enterprise, especially so far as
it affected the interest of the Credit Mobilier Company. On the ninth day of December, 1867, Mr.
C. C. Washburn, of Wisconsin, introduced in the
House a bill to regulate by law the rates of transportation over the Pacific Railroad.

Mr. Ames, as well as others interested in the
Union Pacific road, was opposed to this, and
desired to defeat it. Other measures, apparently
hostile to that company, were subsequently introduced into the House by Mr. Washburn, of Wisconsin, and Mr. Washburne, of Illinois. The
Committee believe that Mr. Ames, in his distribu-
tions of stock, had specially in mind the hostile
efforts of the Messrs. Washburn, and desired to
gain strength to secure their defeat. The reference in one of his letters to "Washburne's move,"
makes this quite apparent.

The offenders were not expelled. Instead,
Congress passed the following:

Whereas, by the report of the special committee
herein, it appears that the acts charged against
members of this House in connection with the
Credit Mobilier of America, occurred more than
five years ago, and long before the election of such
persons to this Congress, two elections by the
people having intervened; and, whereas grave
doubts exist as to the rightful exercise by this
House of its power to expel a member for offenses
committed by such member long before his election
thereto, and not connected with such election:
therefore,

CREDIT MOBILIER

Resolved, That the special committee be discharged from the further consideration of this subject.

Resolved, That the House absolutely condemns the conduct of Oakes Ames, a member of this House from Massachusetts, in seeking to procure Congressional attention to the affairs of a corporation in which he was interested, and whose interest directly depended upon the legislation of Congress, by inducing members of Congress to invest in the stocks of said corporation.

Resolved, That this House absolutely condemns the conduct of James Brooks, a member of this House from New York, for the use of his position as government director of the Union Pacific Railroad, and a member of this House, to procure the assignment to himself or family, of stock in the Credit Mobilier of America, a corporation having a contract with the Union Pacific Railroad, and whose interests depended directly upon the legislation of Congress.

The terms of both Ames and Brooks expired with the fourth of March. Both left their seats broken men and neither survived long, Ames dying at North Easton on May 8, 1873, and Brooks in Washington, on April thirtieth. Colfax retired permanently from public life, the scandal having spoiled the efforts of his friends to place him in the editorial chair of the *New York Tribune,* vacated by Horace Greeley. Henry Wilson died while vice-president. Kelley continued long in Congress, becoming the father of the House. Gar-

[115]

field was elected president, in 1880, the three hundred twenty-nine dollars turning up like Banquo's ghost in his campaign against General W. S. Hancock. The bullet of an assassin ended his life. Logan kept before the public all his days. So did Dawes, who became, as did Logan, a United States senator.

On the summit of the divide, between the oceans, the Pacific Railroad built a monument to the glory of Oliver and Oakes Ames.

Thus we have vindicated the usual American verdict in such matters: "The end justifies the means."

That there was great scandal in the manner in which the road loaded itself upon the West in colossal costs that carried with them high rates for the regions opened and great fortunes for the promoters, seemed to cause far less concern than the political aspects of the revelations. This was not all. The high financing of the Union Pacific was emulated by other railway corporations, without, however, such favorable government support. A legion of new lines were undertaken and financed extravagantly, just as had been done in England a quarter of a century before. The country was railway mad. Every small town wanted a line, and each was sure it would become a metropolis if reached by the magic rails. The result was an immense increment of town, county and state debts, with the proceeds of which reckless promoters played havoc. These usually found their end in that sink of ruin, the New York Stock Exchange, culminating in what is mournfully remembered as the panic of 1873. Seemingly unconscious that it was creating a financial morass, the country in four years had constructed nearly twenty-five thousand miles of railroad, while promoters had come to be in default on some two hundred twenty-nine million dollars of securities.

One of the preliminary symptoms of the coming calamity was the failure of the Brooklyn Trust Company, Saturday, July nineteenth. On the Tuesday before, E. S. Mills, its president, had committed suicide by drowning at Coney Island. He had over-reached himself and used bank funds in promoting the New Haven and Willimantic Railroad, destined to be part of the luckless New England Air Line, to Boston, which in one way or another was to plague financiers for many years. Mills had overdrawn his account one hundred forty-seven thousand dollars and borrowed three hundred fifty thousand dollars more on securities that were worthless, including a big bundle of carpetbag bonds issued by the reconstruction government of Georgia, during the term of Governor Bullock. More than this, with the connivance of Deputy-Treasurer M. T. Rodman, he had dipped his hands into the treasury of the city of Brooklyn for something like two hundred thousand dollars. The suicide was a confession.

THE DREADFUL DECADE

The Trust Company's stockholders rallied to its support, and it was put on its feet. Its doors were soon opened. The incident did not have any alarming effect, as the funds had apparently been used to handle the railroad project. But there was a sort of strain in the financial air, such as is held sometimes to precede an earthquake.

There had been a long and reckless period of speculation on the Stock Exchange, in which the shares of the Pacific Mail Steamship Company, the one American commercial corporation of consequence operating at sea, had been used as a football, with evil consequences to speculators and the concern itself. It owned twenty-eight ships, but had a highly inflated capitalization that made merry markers for Wall Street.

Much degraded, its stock had dropped from two hundred forty to thirty, or thereabouts, when A. B. Stockwell was elected president of the derelict corporation in November, 1871. He had kept a livery stable in Cleveland, Ohio; been a clerk on a Mississippi River steamer and by some chance married an heiress of the Elias Howe Sewing Machine Corporation, of Bridgeport, Connecticut. Quite unknown to the world of finance, he soon blossomed out as "Commodore" Stockwell and revived speculative interest in Pacific Mail, running it up to one hundred three. There was some inexplicable refinancing and a number of mysterious shipwrecks of old and well-insured vessels.

Finally, a bear raid drove the stock back to its old rock bottom, and Stockwell from power. The public, as usual, paid for it. The concern was now in process of reorganization. Besides this, the vast flotations on behalf of railroad building had filled the market with green goods. The Northern Pacific enterprise was under way—five hundred miles toward Oregon having been constructed, with its financing in the hands of the seemingly solid house of Jay Cooke and Company, which, during the summer of 1873, was trying to refund a seven and three-tenths per cent. bond issue at six per cent., while carrying on further financing on behalf of construction. Jay Cooke, who had come from Sandusky, Ohio, to Philadelphia, had made himself a figure as an aid in financing the war and was looked upon as the personification of strength and success.

Whether or not expecting something to break, the *New York World* on Monday, September 1, 1873, printed a page article headed "Wall Street Kings" in which it noted men who had been up and down in recent years, including in its list Leonard W. Jerome, whose brilliant daughter had just married Lord Randolph Churchill, brother of the Duke of Marlborough, and Jay Gould. Sub-heads recited: "A Record of Ruin from Beginning to End. What Speculation Has Done During the Inflation." The article opened with this awesome observation: "There is one man in Wall Street

[119]

to-day whom men watch, and whose name, built upon ruins, carries with it a certain whisper of ruin. He is last of the race of kings." With an evident finger pointing at Jay Gould, the recital continued: "There is one whose nature is best described by the record of what he has done, and by the burden of hatred and dread that, loaded upon him for two and one-half years, has not turned him one hair from any place that promised him gain and the most bitter ruin for his chance opponents. They that curse him do not do it blindly, but as cursing one who massacres after victory."

The second prelude to the panic came on Saturday, September 13, 1873, when the old-established house of Kenyon, Cox and Company closed its doors. The venerable and expert Daniel Drew was one of the partners. The failure was not caused by operations on the Exchange, but by over-indorsement by Drew, Cox and the firm, of the notes of the Canada Southern Railway. They had expected to cover themselves by the sale of five million dollars in bonds, which had failed to find a market, and were involved for several millions. On the Monday previous, the New York Warehouse and Security Company had gone under, because of loans out to the extent of one million, two hundred thousand dollars, which it could not collect. Monday, the fifteenth, saw a quiet market. The next day, the New York, Oswego and Midland allowed its paper to go to protest. There was more paper than railroad in its affairs, but this did not jar the market perceptibly. Money, however, was high. This the financial writers laid to a considerable speculation in gold which had been going on for some time, with the usual accumulation of shorts, who were now being forced to pay for their temerity in trifling with the metal.

The gold "shorts" were not alone, however. The sinister Jay Gould had been selling Western Union short at eighty-eight, or thereabouts. This was his favorite stock, and in time, he controlled it. Floods of rumors were set afloat to ease the shorts, but they made no dent in the general run of values.

On the morning of September eighteenth, the market opened feverishly but with no hint of what was to happen later in the day. There was no demand for railway stocks, and gold was advancing. The Treasury Department was ready to unloose one million, five hundred thousand dollars, but held it back owing to the uncertainty of price. At ten minutes after twelve, an announcement came that threw the country, as well as the Exchange, off its financial feet. Jay Cooke and Company had suspended. The Northern Pacific had proved too much of a load. The story was thus briefly told: "Messrs. Jay Cooke and Company have announced their suspension in consequence of large advances made to sustain their Philadelphia house and a heavy draft upon their own deposits. It is hoped the suspension will be only temporary."

In ten minutes, Western Union had dropped ten points, filling the short Gould pockets. Other securities were shorn of their values in rapid disorder. The whole country, seemingly, sought to throw its holdings into the hopper.

Other failures followed fast. Fisk and Hatch went under, followed by Richard Schell, a Vanderbilt broker, and Robinson and Suydam. E. W. Clark and Company, in Philadelphia, closed their doors, while the parent house of Jay Cooke, in the Quaker City, followed suit. In Washington, Fant, Washington and Company suspended. Fant was the man who had failed to take up the Credit Mobilier stock, and so made the McComb move possible. A run started on the First National Bank in Washington, of which Jay Cooke's brother was the head, and the bank shut its doors under the protection of the police. The market closed rather calmly, but the next day the extent of the crash began to make itself felt. Jacob Little and Company, E. D. Randolph and Company, George B. Alley and Company, W. H. Warren and Company, Greenleaf, Norris and Company, Thomas Reed and Company, Whittemore and Anderson, Beers and Edwards, Eugene J. Jackson, White, De Freites and Rathbone, A. M. Kidder and Company, Smith and Seaver, Theodore Bendall, Hay and Warner, Day and Morse, Vernam and Hoy, Fitch and Company, and Washington E. Commor went to the wall. It was another Black Friday, indeed, with a great fall of rain from a gloomy sky that well matched the darkness underneath. Wall and Broad Streets were jammed with people, wild with excitement and fearful of the future. Gold rose to one hundred twelve and one-half.

Saturday, the situation did not improve. Instead, more failures followed, the victims being Ketchum and Belknap, Taussig, Fisher and Company, C. G. White, Williams and Bostwick, Peter M. Myers and Company, Lawrence Josephs, Fearing and Dillinger, Saxe and Rogers, Brown, Wadsworth and Company, Miller and Walsh and Edmund Haight and Company. These were small items against the breaking of the banks which also began. The Union Trust Company, the Bank of the Commonwealth and the National Trust Company, went under on this same evil day. In the case of the Union Trust Company, its secretary, C. T. Carlton, was found a defaulter in three hundred fifty thousand dollars. The National Trust called its suspension a "precaution." The Commonwealth was frankly broke, an overdraft from Edmund Haight and Company, which got past the paying teller, giving the *coup de grace,* which, starting the withdrawal of one million dollars in a "run," did the business.

These failures caused another bad break in stocks. To stop the panicky selling the Stock Exchange closed its doors after a short session, *sine die.* Prices were utterly demoralized. Even

[123]

Gould quit buying on the breaks. A block of Western Union was offered for forty-five, about half its value, and went unsold.

Gould was interviewed by the *World,* and his remarks were printed on Monday, September twenty-second. He thought the trouble was due to heavy advances made by the banks for the construction of railroads that could never pay a cent in return, and "the bad financial managing of the government." To this, he added the usual "lack of confidence," as a final explanation. The government, for one thing, thanks to the action of the sub-treasury in New York, had failed to buy its bonds as offered, though funds were in hand. This was corrected on Monday when $3,339,150 worth were purchased. The issue of five million dollars in Clearing House certificates also helped matters.

The situation was steadied, but not healed. On Tuesday, September twenty-third, Henry Clews and Company suspended. His was the only failure of the day. Frightened depositors now began demanding their money of the savings banks, and slight runs followed. Wednesday the failure of Howes and Macy, a substantial house, was announced. Far-reaching effects began. The State Bank of New Brunswick, New Jersey, failed, and the defalcation of a Hoboken savings bank official, who had traded with Fisk and Hatch, became known.

Railway building was checked at once. The

Rogers' works in Paterson, builders of locomotives, laid off one thousand hands, the forerunner of what was to be a long period of unemployment throughout the land, led by manufacturers of railroad supplies all over the country.

The government continued to buy bonds—up to September twenty-ninth, taking over fourteen million dollars' worth, and President Grant promised the banks the use of forty-four million dollars in the Treasury reserve. Currency, however, was at a premium of three and one-half per cent. against certified checks, and many firms could not get cash for payrolls, causing distress in manufacturing centers. Gold went up to one hundred fourteen.

The Stock Exchange reopened for business on September thirtieth, without causing any excitement, and resumed all its functions, legitimate and otherwise. On October first, the government decided to release three million dollars in gold to relieve the monetary strain. It carried a premium on that date of seven and one-half cents over currency value per dollar. The panic was over, but its consequences were not.

The day after the Exchange reopened its doors, Northrup and Chick, a banking and brokerage concern, went out of existence. Currency continued at a premium. George Bird Grinnell and Company (Joseph C. Williams) were expelled from the Stock Exchange for failing to meet their obligations, and then suspended business. Paterson and Company, a considerable factor in the whole-sale dry-goods trade, went under. Savings banks, overloaded with railway securities, began to fail, one of the earliest being the City Savings Bank of Washington. Private bankers over the country also began closing down. One of the first firms to go was Harshman and Gorman of Dayton, Ohio. Cincinnati banks suspended payments in currency and did not resume the practise until October thirteenth. On the fourteenth, a great wave of selling at broken prices engulfed the Stock Exchange, with resulting losses in values. Western Union, which had touched the seventies, dropped to forty-nine, to the evident profit of Jay Gould. There were some minor failures, William Hoge and Company, W. M. Whittemore and Company, Boyd, Vincent and Company and C. H. Pierce and Company being the victims. The payment, on the fifteenth, of a New York Central dividend amounting to three million, six hundred thousand dollars, steadied things for the moment. Charles H. Phelps, Deputy State Treasurer of New York, was found short three hundred thousand dollars and put under arrest after a flight from Albany to Jersey City. Failures continued on the Stock Exchange, the next victims being E. W. and J. P. Converse.

The use of unsound currency, which produced the demoralization, had its origin in the exigencies of the Civil War. When the conflict between the states broke out with the bombardment of Fort Sumter, April 12, 1861, the country was as poorly equipped financially as it was in trained army and munitions. Its expenses had been small, and these were readily met with the modest amount of specie that came in through the customs. The country itself stumbled along on gold from California, coined at the mints for a small seigniorage, and a very limited amount of silver handled in the same way, plus the notes of varying value of some one hundred and forty state banks. These last had replaced a vast amount of "wild-cat" currency, issued to any one who would take it, by banks that came to life in the boom times of the 'thirties.

Facing financial, as well as other crises, the Congress, February 28, 1862, passed what was called a Legal Tender Act, by which it authorized the issue of government notes—"greenbacks," as they became known, because of their color—with which it could by fiat pay its own bills, while at the same time insisting upon receiving its revenues in gold.

This established a form of squeezing that was to cost the nation dear. It did not suffice to relieve the stress and Congress accepted a National Bank system, devised by George S. Coe, long head of the American Exchange National Bank, New York, by which it was able to produce more currency, and sell its bonds. Briefly, the banks bought bonds, deposited them in the Treasury and were allowed to issue notes up to ninety per cent. of the value of the securities so sequestrated.

This proved to be a workable device, and was popular with bankers, as it gave them a chance to "eat their cake and have it," while the bonds were redeemable in gold. The state banks, which were flourishing nicely by selling their gold at a premium and putting out notes, were forbidden the latter practise, and the government alone was left in a position to cheat its citizens.

This it proceeded to do with energy, until it had issued seven hundred thirty-seven million dollars in greenbacks. Many contractors refused to accept the currency, arguing that, as the Treasury insisted on having its revenues in gold, it should pay out with the same money. The soldiers in the field had no such recourse. They had to take the stuff. So money became cheap—a dollar, at one time, meaning thirty-seven cents—which made prices high. It is one of the curiosities of the human mind that, instead of hastening to correct such a condition, the people will cling to it. Be it observed parenthetically, in view of the agitation for fiat money that was to follow and vex the country for a quarter of a century, that there is no way for such money to reach the pockets of the people save through a deficit in the revenues of government. When its budgets balanced, it had no need to issue notes any more than an individual. Just how such "hayseed" financiers as Blanton

Duncan, James B. Weaver and Solon Chase, who led the greenback hosts, expected the currency to reach the pockets of the people, save through getting them deeper into debt, was never made clear.

Following the close of the war, the Treasury began, as its revenues steadied, to retire the fiat notes. By the time General Grant became president, March 4, 1869, some one hundred forty million dollars had been retired, not to the gratitude but to the disgust of the country. Contraction was called a crime—and in the interest of bankers. The country had been on a splendid debauch and did not want to taper off. It was not possible to convince the people at large that "things equal to the same things are equal to each other."

The initial test of public temper came early in Grant's administration, when what were known as the five-twenty bonds, the first issued to finance the war, fell due. They had been made redeemable on demand in five years, but could be kept twenty years by the holder, if he so desired. They were payable in gold, then selling at one hundred thirty. Senator John Sherman, of Ohio, was then, as always, an outstanding figure in national financing. When this question arose, his own state originated what became known as the "Ohio idea," which, in brief, was to pay the bonds in greenbacks, though their owners had paid gold for them, and had been promised gold in return. But the bond-holders had been paid interest in gold bought at a premium at the expense of the country at large, so their sufferings, even had the Ohio idea prevailed, would have been more apparent than real. There was, however, some equivocation in the legal tender act. It did seem that money which the government issued to pay soldiers ought to be good enough to pay bondholders. The matter was made an issue before the United States Supreme Court, which in a four to three decision, handed down February 7, 1874, declared that the act "impaired the obligations of contracts and was inconsistent with the spirit of the Constitution." The man who read the opinion was Chief Justice Salmon P. Chase, who, as secretary of the treasury, had helped force through the Legal Tender Act. He explained that in the confusion of war times, expediency sometimes over-ruled ethics.

The stream of paper dammed up, another began flooding the country with a "hard" money that brought great profit to its producers. The silver mines of the Comstock lode in Nevada were pouring out tons of the white metal, which enjoyed a basic parity. By having it coined and then exchanging it for greenbacks, the mine owners flourished amazingly. In the period previous to the war, silver, at a ratio of sixteen to one, fixed by the Act of 1834, and amended by that of 1837, was more valuable than gold, and remained practically out of use as currency. The Nevada output of silver of the post-war period imperiled the national finances, as well as the value of the currency. As a result, Congress, in 1873, after spending three years on the subject, which had been brought to its attention by George S. Boutwell, Secretary of the Treasury, demonetized silver for all but fractional coinage. This became known later as the celebrated "Crime of 1873," a war-cry in the campaign of 1896.

Failures followed the acute period with continuing ill-consequences on trade and employment. The great cotton manufacturing concern of A. and W. Sprague, of Rhode Island, went under. William Sprague, the junior in the firm, had been governor of the state and had married Kate Chase, the beautiful and intellectual daughter of the chief justice. The crash was colossal and brought ruin to many besides the Spragues.

Defalcations were also numerous. The greatest of them was one of eight hundred thousand dollars taken by E. J. Blake, president of the Mercantile Bank of New York, from its coffers, to float the Domestic Sewing Machine Company. The panic caught many a good man with his hands in other people's pockets.

Taxes fell into arrears, mortgages were foreclosed, and the laboring classes went hungry. The winter of 1874 was one of the dreariest in the history of the land. Soup-kitchens had to be established in the cities. In New York many thousands were without employment. Nor was this condition temporary. It was to endure many months.

The hasty rush of settlers that anticipated the coming of railroads into the trans-Mississippi region produced great hardship. Living in sod-houses on wind-swept plains, summer and winter alike, tried the pioneers severely. Plagues of grasshoppers, chinch bugs and the army worm swept away their crops, and the diseases of a newly settled section added to their misery and despair. The Kansas and Nebraska prairies certainly avenged themselves on the intruding settlers. Besides this, markets were poor, and money was incredibly hard to obtain, save at usurious interest and on exacting terms. Quite naturally, recalling the flush times of inflation, the perturbed and unfortunate people turned again to the greenback for relief. The sound and able Boutwell had left the Treasury to become senator from Massachusetts, and his place had been badly filled by W. A. Richardson, from the same state, a man of inferior capacity and no real idea of financial administration. When Congress assembled in December, 1873, all the quacks were busy. More than three score of measures were proposed to remedy the situation by law. Fortunately, Senator John Sherman, of Ohio, was chairman of the Senate Finance Committee, and the crop of wild oats came into his hands for threshing. His committee propounded a resolution looking rightly to the early resumption of specie payments as a remedy. This was met by a measure fathered by Senator Thomas W. Ferry, of Michigan, calling for renewed inflation. Senators Oliver P. Morton, of Indiana, and John A. Logan, of Illinois, stood with him on the unsound side. Ferry wished to issue one hundred million dollars in greenbacks, quite unconscious that the only way they could get into circulation was by default in revenue, or by buying and locking up silver bullion, both evil ways. Morton would have been content with forty-four million dollars, to be added to the Treasury reserve, another futility, so far as the public was concerned.

Secretary Richardson, finding a shortage in his supply of money, due to a drop in revenue receipts, put out four million dollars in greenbacks. The revenues continuing to run low, he met the deficit with more fiats, until by January 10, 1874, he had added twenty-six million dollars to the country's supply of notes. Sherman, Allen G. Thurman, his Democratic colleague from Ohio, and Carl Schurz, of Missouri, were certain that Richardson's action was illegal, having been performed without the sanction of Congress. A four-months debate on the Ferry Bill resulted. This measure, in final form, lifted the reserve to four hundred million dollars in paper. It had been down to three hundred fifty-six million dollars. Richardson's issues had raised it to three hundred eighty-two million dollars, so the extra inflation was eighteen million dollars, plus the legalizing of the twenty-six million dollars. It passed the Senate, April 6, 1874, twenty-nine to twenty-four; the House on April fourteenth, by one hundred forty to one hundred two.

The responsibility now became the president's, and he met it manfully. Enormous party pressure was put upon him from the West to save it by signing the bill. The East rather supposed he would. The opinion of the South was of no consequence. He stood at the parting of the ways, but here, as on all great occasions where courage was required and no friendship involved, his nerve did not fail. Struggling with the specious argument that this was not truly, inflation, but merely restoring a former condition, he wrote the draft of a message justifying the measure, but when he read it over, he saw that it was unsound and specious. Then he flung it aside and vetoed the bill, one of the bravest acts in executive history.

Following up the advantage gained by the veto, which was sustained, Senator Sherman brought forward an Act for the Resumption of Specie Payments. It provided for the retirement of shinplasters, or the fractional currency notes, and for the coinage of small units under one dollar in silver—ten, twenty-five and fifty-cent pieces; for the reduction of the greenback supply as fast as national banks issued their notes on a ratio of eighty to one hundred, and until the greenbacks were cut to three hundred million dollars. Finally, the measure provided for actual resumption on January 1, 1879, and bonds were authorized to secure the needed gold. This passed the Senate December 21, 1874, by thirty-two to fourteen. It was an open question whether the bill barred re-issue of the retired one hundred million dollars, and the sound-money Democrats, together with Carl Schurz, were against it for that reason, though Schurz finally voted for it. The House passed it, January 14, 1875, by a vote of one hundred thirty-six to ninety-eight. So far as Congress was concerned, the greenback peril was over. Not so in regard to the country. There arose forthwith a greenback party that was to make a great deal of noise before its voice was stilled.

The "greenbackers," as they were called, flourished mightily in the West among one hundred per cent. Americans, and reflexed into far-eastern Maine where they became formidable in 1878 and 1879, under the leadership of Solon Chase, a former Republican living at Chase's Mills, a hamlet of nine houses and a sawmill in the town of Turner. He worked up a great following. By fusion with the Democrats, who had been sorely depressed since copperhead days, the legislature of Maine was captured, and the governorship, twice: once from the Republicans in the legislature who preferred Doctor Alonzo B. Garcelon to a greenbacker, and once by the outright election of General Harris M. Plaisted. Indeed, Plaisted's success in the September election of 1880 in Maine, rallied financial interests to the support of James A. Garfield and had much to do with defeating General Winfield Scott Hancock for the presidency. This was the high tide of the heresy which backed James B. Weaver for president, until the time when it took refuge in populism and free silver.

CHAPTER IV

THE VIRGINIUS AFFAIR

Capture of the Filibuster by the Tornado—Shooting of Captain
Joseph B. Fry and His Companions—Prelude to Cuban Freedom—
American Indignation—No Requital Until 1898.

FOLLOWING the panic of 1873, with its trail of
poverty and despair, came a tragedy that wrung
the hearts of Americans as none ever had before,
and that remains memorable. In 1869, the people
of Cuba, tired of a brutal and costly rule, had risen
in revolt against Spain under the leadership of
Manuel Céspedes and Miguel Aldama, both men
of noble character and high qualities. Aldama was
exceedingly wealthy. His home at the head of
the Prado was the most palatial in Havana.
Céspedes had the position of a leading citizen. A
junta, headed by Aldama, had its headquarters in
New York, from which it financed the rebellion
and sent arms, ammunition and recruits to the now
faithless "Everfaithful Isle."

This required the fitting out of filibustering
expeditions, the participants in which took desperate chances from the moment they enlisted. The
War between the States had many adventurous
leftovers, and the state of American commerce was

[137]

low. The whale fishery had been destroyed by the Confederate cruisers, and other shipping had suffered severely from the same cause, while many vessels had been placed under foreign flags from which laws passed by an unintelligent Congress prevented their return. Besides, many men who had served the Confederacy were out of jobs. One of these was Captain Joseph B. Fry. He was a Floridan by birth (though his ancestors were from Greenwich, Rhode Island) who had been given a midshipman's warrant in the United States Navy and who had later reached the rank of lieutenant. Having charge of the Eighth Lighthouse District, he was living in Louisiana, when, on January 26, 1861, that state seceded from the Union. He forwarded his resignation to Washington and entered the Confederate service. He had a lively experience on western rivers and wound up his career on the *Morgan,* at Mobile, where Farragut's fleet captured the vessel in one of the most famous sea fights on record.

Paroled, he saw no more service, and after the war, resided in New Orleans, engaging in various unremunerative occupations, which took but poor care of a wife and three children.

In July, 1873, Captain Fry came to New York seeking employment. He wanted to secure command of an ocean steamer, and hunting about, came in contact with Manuel Quesada, chief of the Cuban Junta, who offered him the command of a

Joseph Fry

vessel then lying in the harbor of Kingston, Jamaica, whence she was expected to make some landing in Cuba. The vessel was a Clyde-built craft, constructed for blockade running during the war. Fry had known her of old as the *Virgin,* for she had carried cotton out of Mobile to Havana and had done duty as a dispatch boat during Farragut's siege. She had been sold by the government to American owners, tragically renamed *Virginius,* and on September 25, 1870, was regularly registered at the New York Custom House, taking out papers for a Venezuela port, but never making it. Instead she landed Quesada and twenty-one compatriots in Cuba. This was on June 21, 1871. Her officers were Americans, and blockade running was not a crime, even when caught. Later she was cornered at Colon by the Spanish cruiser *Bazen,* whose captain announced his purpose to take her when she left her anchorage. The U. S. S. *Kansas* was in port and carefully conducted the craft out of range on July first, remaining off the harbor until the *Virginius* dropped below the skyline, while the *Canandaigua* remained in harbor to keep the Spaniard company. Naturally, the don kept his mud-hook down. The *Virginius* then made a second landing and deposited a large lot of arms where they were more needed.

So badly off was Captain Fry that he undertook the risky command for one hundred fifty dollars per month. The mail steamer *Atlas* carried the adventurers and a number of Cubans to Jamaica on October 4, 1873. Here Fry took command of the ship on arrival. Her history was well-known, and Kingston, familiar with the game, was very friendly. Ten hospitable days followed, and the captain reciprocated with a ball on board ship the night before making sail. Another former Confederate was along, General Washington A. C. Ryan, who wrote of these last happy hours: "Since our arrival we have had a splendid time, feast after feast, and ball after ball. The first ball was given by the Peruvian Minister in honor of General Varona and myself. All the fashion and wealth of the place was present. Mr. [Manuel] Govin, General Cordova and Judge Ticheborn gave the others, and joyous they were."

Ticheborn was the United States consul who cleared the *Virginius,* and she sailed October twenty-third for Port au Prince, where she took on a cargo of arms and supplies for the Cubans, together with sundry additions to her company, which now numbered one hundred fifty-five men. The Spanish consul protested, and she was ordered to sea under escort of a Haitian gunboat.

Her movements were being followed by Spain, and the Spanish consul at Kingston warned the authorities at Havana of her whereabouts. As a result the cruiser *Tornado,* Commander Dionisio Castillo, was sent from Santiago de Cuba to seek her out. The *Tornado* had been a blockade runner, built in the same Clyde yard as the former *Virgin.*

THE VIRGINIUS AFFAIR

The *Tornado* left Santiago on the twenty-ninth of October and cruised through the night between that point and Cape Cruz, yet observed nothing. During the day she lay easily under sail, yet caught no sight of the expected ship. The night of the thirtieth revealed nothing, but at daybreak smoke was seen indicating a steamer taking the course for Jamaica. For some eighteen miles the *Tornado* followed the trail, trying to make out the stranger. Rightly supposing from her course that this was the *Virginius,* Castillo now got up steam. The *Virginius* recognized her pursuer and headed for Point Morante.

When the people on the *Virginius* first sighted the *Tornado* as she was loafing under sail, it did not seem to occur to Fry or his associates that here was an enemy. It was two hours before smoke poured from her stack and it began to dawn on the filibusters that trouble was ahead. The fires on the *Virginius* were low as she was idling to await a favorable moment for making a landing. It was soon evident that the *Tornado* meant business, for flames leaped from her funnel in response to the fervid firing below.

And so now the *Virginius* began a corresponding effort to make steam, throwing hams, bacon and oil into her furnaces. This was of no avail, as her clumsy side-wheels could propel her at the best no more than eight knots per hour, and she had not been docked for fifteen months. The

Tornado was no lightning express, but she could beat that. The cannon were thrown over to lighten ship, but still the Spaniard gained. Arms, ammunition and stores followed. Still the pursuer crept up. Then the sun set, and there was hope that night would save them, but it was too late. The flames from the twin stacks of the *Virginius* kept her in view and at nine o'clock the *Tornado* came within gunshot and opened fire. The first shot went under the mark. The lights of Jamaica were in sight, and it seemed certain that the ship was safe. Other shots followed—five in all. One wrecked the smoke-stack of the *Virginius,* and she was brought to. As all the arms and ammunition had been jettisoned, there was no means of resistance at hand. Some of the Cubans on board wished to blow up the ship, being quite aware of their probable fate at Spanish hands. To this Fry would not listen. "I want to save you," he said. "This is an American ship; she has American colors and American papers; an American captain and an American crew." Upon this thought, he placed what proved to be a vain reliance, though the *Virginius* was in English waters and presumably safe.

Soon two armed boats were alongside, commanded respectively by Midshipman Don Angel Ortiz Monastario and Don Enrique Pardo. The vessel was boarded, seized, and all hands proclaimed prisoners, though nothing contraband was found, and Fry exhibited papers showing her to be a passenger vessel under charter for Port Limon, Costa Rica. He protested the seizure and invited the Spaniards to observe that he was under the American flag, the response to which was an order to haul it down. This was done, and the beautiful banner trampled upon and defiled. In its place rose the sinister standard of Spain.

"I do not care what flag you carry," said Ortiz, the officer in command of the boats. "You are a pirate and all are prisoners."

Fry replied that "if his men were armed, there would be no such treatment of his flag." This only brought sneers in reply. The passengers and crew were mustered aft and searched. They were deprived of all their valuables and spare clothing. Fry and nine others were bound and locked in the cabin. The remaining prisoners were taken to the *Tornado* and both vessels steered for Santiago de Cuba. "The enthusiasm of the crew simply baffled description," reported Castillo, "when success crowned our efforts." He also assured the authorities at Havana that "the prisoners were treated with such consideration as their character deserved and the necessity for their safe keeping demanded," which leaves much to be implied. The *Tornado* and her captives reached Santiago at five o'clock on the evening of November first, when, as Castillo further observes: "Our arrival was made the signal of a general outburst of patriotic enthusiasm." He then made his report to Juan N. Burriel, the captain-general, and ended it with the comment that "what must now follow has to be dictated by the officers of justice."

The ship, according to a report made by Midshipman Ortiz, "was in a very lamentable condition." He continues:

"The furnaces were not only dirty because of the considerable quantity of grease and hams with which they had been fed, but also the machinery and the packing were in bad condition; for they had suffered much during the chase. The vessel was taking a considerable quantity of water at a badly calked point, which is toward the prow and below the water-line generally, on account of the bad condition of the bottom; for she had labored much during the chase. It not being possible to reach the forward section of the ship for want of means of communication, the rest of her and the machinery were attended to. Her aspect was truly repugnant. She was not only full of grease and broken boxes, that served as packing to the rest of the cargo, but also in a notably abandoned condition. The dead angle of the porthole was very much damaged, because from this place the cargo of arms and ammunition was thrown into the water, to do which they had mounted a block and pulley that as yet remained in the same place. The cabin was in disorder, trunks open, clothes thrown about, portmanteaus entirely destroyed, and in all parts of the ship unmistakable signs that everything of any value had been thrown into the water. Not only were there open arm-boxes there, but even cartridges of rifle and revolver, boxes of leather, belts, machetes and insurgent cockades. Under the coal there are barrels, but it has not been possible for me to divert the men's attention to examine them, because I could not neglect guard duty, which has been strictly attended to, without intermission. Saddles, insurgent buttons and a portion of papers and effects that were scattered about in all directions, have been gathered up by my orders."

The patriotic demonstration noted by Castillo did not come from the people of Santiago de Cuba, whose hearts sank when they saw the *Tornado* come in with her prize. The cheers were from the throats of the so-called "Spanish Volunteers," who, like the Tories of the American Revolution, were far more inimical to the patriots than the soldiers of Spain. Fry had not been much alarmed as to consequences, recalling the easy way of dealing with captured blockaders during the Civil War in the states, but he now took fright. To Leopold Rizo, his interpreter, he said: "I fear no mercy will be shown us. Should you escape, go to my friends and family in New Orleans. Be to my wife as a son, in telling her of my last moments. If I die, it will be for the Cuban cause."

His forebodings came true without delay. The judicial authorities did not act. Instead, a court-martial was held on board the *Tornado* the next day, November second, when the captives were tried as pirates, and a sealed verdict sent to Burriel.

[145]

Sunday afternoon following, all of the *Virginius'* company were landed and taken to prison, pinioned and handcuffed, with the exception of General Washington A. C. Ryan, General Jesus del Sol, General Bernabé Varona and General Pedro Céspedes, who were spared the indignity. These four distinguished and gallant men were taken from jail at a quarter to seven on Tuesday morning, November fifth, and escorted to the place of execution at the municipal slaughter-yard, a ten-minute walk. Ryan wore a blue shirt over his white garment, and on his breast, the silver star of the republic he was trying to establish. Soldier-of-fortune-like, he smoked a cigar nonchalantly and did not toss it away until the moment he was before the firing squad of Volunteers.

Alfred N. Young, the American Consul, was absent from his post, and E. G. Schmitt, the vice-consul, was rebuffed by Burriel and a guard placed around the consulate. The cable and telegraph office was also guarded to prevent the sending of any messages. Word of the capture had reached America and General Daniel E. Sickles, our minister at Madrid, had been asked to intercede with the Spanish Government on behalf of the prisoners. He reported that Emilio Castelar, President, (Spain was then a republic) had promised that nothing abrupt would be done, and Washington was resting under this assurance. So the execution went on unhampered. Céspedes and

Del Sol were forced to kneel and be shot in the
back. Ryan and Varona tried to stand and face
the fire like soldiers. They were knocked down
and butchered, a Spanish officer running Ryan
through with his sword. Some cavalrymen then
rode their horses over the corpses and a mob was
let loose, which cut off the heads of the murdered
generals and carried them about the streets on
pikes in a triumphant procession. Fifteen regular
Spanish officers, who had been prisoners under
Varona, begged Burriel to stay the execution, but
the brute refused.

Foreign ships were held in the harbor to prevent the news from leaking out. The consuls were
told that Burriel was acting on his own responsibility and did not even intend to inform Madrid.
This was true. George W. Sherman, an American, who saw the horror and tried to make some
sketches, was arrested and kept three days in
duress. The bodies, mutilated beyond recognition,
were carted to a swamp and thrown into a ditch.

Theodore Brooks, the British Vice-Consul, had
also made a protest on behalf of some sixteen
Englishmen in the fated company. Burriel declined to listen to him. On the afternoon of the
fifth Vice-Consul Schmitt was allowed to visit
Captain Fry with the evident knowledge that he
was soon to be executed. At two o'clock, Fry
wrote and filed a formal protest against the proceedings in these terms:

That he was the master of the American
steamer *Virginius,* which had all her papers in
complete order, especially the register of the
steamer, the crew list and articles, passenger list,
clearance from Kingston, as also dispatch from the
custom house, etc. Sailed on the twenty-third of
October, 1873, with all his crew and about one hundred and eight passengers; after a few hours at
sea, sprung a leak, and put into Port Haytien for
repairs. Sailed from the port of Cuimit, of that
island, on the thirtieth day of October, and while
between the Islands of Cuba and Jamaica, about
twenty miles or more from Cuba, was chased by a
steamer, and overtaken and captured about eighteen miles north of Morante Point, east end of the
Island of Jamaica, about ten o'clock at night, the
Spanish vessel previously firing several shots over
the *Virginius,* and compelling them to surrender.
The steamer was then taken charge of by a board-
ing officer, who stated that he did so on his own
responsibility, knowing her to be an American
vessel, and under the protection of the flag of the
United States of America. The master, Joseph
Fry, with the crew and passengers, was placed
under guard, and all brought into the port of
Santiago de Cuba on the first day of November.
On the evening of the same day, after having
delivered over all the papers belonging to the
Virginius, he was refused permission to apply to
his consul for aid and protection, and this was only
granted him after being condemned to death, with
the major part of his crew, under no known public
law or pretext; and as Captain Fry was hurried to
make his preparations for death, he could make no
further statement, but declare that the foregoing

is his true declaration, which he signed in jail, at two o'clock, on the seventh of November, 1873, two hours previous to his execution.

Vice-Consul Schmitt indorsed this protest, as did the British and some other consuls, but to no purpose. Two hours later, Captain Fry and thirty-six members of the crew—William Baynard, first mate; James Flood, second mate; J. C. Harris, John Posa, B. P. Chamberlain, William Rose, Ignacio Dueñas, Antonio Deloyo, José Manuel Ferran, Ramon Lawamendi, Eusebio Gariza, Edward Day, J. S. Trujillo, Jack Williamson, Porfirio Coroison, P. Alfaro, Thomas Grigg, Frank Good, Paul Kuner, Bamey Herald, Samuel Card, John Brown, Alfred Haisel, W. J. Prince, George Thomas, Ezekiel Durham, Thomas Walter Williams, Simon Broome, Leopold Larose, A. Arsi, John Stewart, Henry Bond, George Thompson, James Samuel, Henry Frank, and James Read—were taken from jail and marched in a column of fours to the place of execution. Here is the account of what followed, from an eye-witness:

The victims were ranged facing the wall, and at a sufficient distance from it to give them room to fall forward. Captain Fry having asked for a glass of water, one was handed him by Charles Bell, the steward of the *Morning Star*. Fry then walked from the end of the line to the center and calmly awaited his fate. He was the only man who

dropped dead at the first volley, notwithstanding
that the firing party were but ten feet away. Then
ensued a horrible scene. The Spanish butchers
advanced to where the wounded men lay writhing
and moaning in agony, and, placing the muzzles
of their guns in some instances into the mouths of
their victims, pulled the triggers, shattering their
heads into fragments. Others of the dying men
grasped the weapons thrust at them with a despair-
ing clutch, and shot after shot was poured into
their bodies before death quieted them.

The next day, November eighth, twelve of the
Cuban passengers went the same way to their
deaths.* Now it happened that although guarded,
the English operator in the cable office had some
hours before ticked three words to Jamaica:
"They are murdering ——" when he was knocked
down with the butt of a musket. The words
chilled Kingston. Admiral A. F. De Horsey, in
command of the naval station, cabled Burriel to
delay further executions until the *Niobe* could
reach the scene, bespeaking the friendly relations
between England and Spain. Burriel replied: "I
do not possess the authority to accede to the peti-
tion you send. The law must be fulfilled."

This message came late in the evening and the
Niobe, Captain Sir Lambton Lorraine, slipped
her moorings at midnight and flew out of the har-

---

*These were Augustine Santa Rosa, Eumineo Quesada, Colonel
Juan Aguerro, Enrique Castellanos, Arturo L. Mola, Augustin
Varona, Guillermo Volls, José Boite, Salvador Penedo, Justo Con-
suegra, Francisco Parrapi a, and José Otero.

bor for Santiago de Cuba. Reaching that port, Lorraine did not stop to anchor, but jumping into a boat from the still moving ship, made for shore, leaving his executive officer to clear for action while he served notice on Burriel, on behalf of sixteen English among the captives, that the executions must cease. He also said that in the absence of an American warship he would represent the United States and protect its citizens, as well as those of English birth.

Originally all had been doomed to swing at the yard-arm of the *Tornado*, but Captain Castillo had no stomach for such work and at his behest the condemned were ordered shot. There was further mitigation, due to Castillo. Knight, the engineer, and three others were to be imprisoned for life; thirteen minors were to be imprisoned for from four to eight years. This left eighty-five more to die, had Lorraine not interfered.

Rumors of the shooting of Ryan, Varona, Céspedes and Del Sol began to reach the United States on November seventh. It caused no great commotion except among the members of the Cuban colony in New York. The government was moving with its customary slowness and had relied on the Madrid assurance. The slaughter of Ryan and his companions did not become definitely known until November twelfth—the news was published in the New York morning papers of the thirteenth.

This roused public feeling to a boiling point.

The country had been sore on the subject of Cuba since Crittenden and fifty of his companions had been executed with Lopez at Havana in 1851. The wave of wrath was nation-wide. President Grant, however, had seen enough of war and went about his task of dealing with the matter lethargically. True, warships were sent to Cuba and a prodigious fuss made, but no reparations were ever exacted from Spain beyond the return of the *Virginius* and the release of the remaining one hundred and two prisoners. There was some reason for not being more exacting. The Castelar Government was being assailed at home as well as in Cuba. Don Carlos, the Bourbon pretender, was waging war to destroy the republic and capture the throne. The Carlists were strong among the Spanish Volunteers who were largely responsible for the executions. It seemed to Grant and Hamilton Fish, his secretary, that no real responsibility in the matter rested with the Spanish Government.

The *Virginius* had been sent to Havana, and on the morning of December 12, 1873, she gave lines to a tugboat and under escort of the Spanish warship *Isabella la Catollica* was towed to Bahia Honda and there delivered to the U. S. S. *Dispatch,* which took the unlucky ship to the Dry Tortugas. Here she was taken in tow by the U. S. S. *Ossipee,* Commander John Watters, to be delivered at New York for examination and further inquiry into her status. The ships sailed on the nineteenth of December. Leaks soon developed under the strain of rough weather, until off Cape Fear, on Christmas Day, she was abandoned and soon sank, not without a suspicion that auger holes in her hull assisted in the calamity as a way out of an awkward situation, when it came time for Spain to ask questions. The *Ossipee* reached New York on December thirtieth. The prisoners were turned over to Commander D. L. Braine of the *Juniata* on December 18, 1873, and brought to New York, where they arrived December twenty-eighth. So the terrible incident ended. President Grant gave this account of his proceedings in a special message sent to Congress in January:

In my message of December last, I gave reason to expect that when the full and accurate text of the correspondence relating to the *Virginius,* which had been telegraphed in cipher, should be received, the papers concerning the capture of the vessel, the execution of a part of its passengers and crew, and the restoration of the ship and the survivors, would be transmitted to Congress.

In compliance with the expectations then held out, I now transmit the papers and correspondence on that subject.

On the twenty-sixth of September, 1870, the *Virginius* was registered in the custom house at New York, as the property of a citizen of the United States, he having first made oath, as required by law, that he was the true and only owner of the said vessel, and that there was no subject or citizen of any foreign prince or state, directly or indirectly, by way of trust, confidence, or otherwise, interested therein. Having complied with the requisites of the statute in that behalf, she cleared, in the usual way, for the port of Curaçoa, and on or about the fourth of October, 1870, sailed for that port.

It is not disputed that she made the voyage according to her clearance, nor that from that day to this she has not returned within the territorial jurisdiction of the United States. It is also understood that she preserved her American papers, and that when within foreign ports she made the practise of putting forth a claim to American nationality, which was recognized by the authorities at such ports. When, therefore, she left the port of Kingston in October last, under the flag of the United States, she would appear to have had, against all powers except the United States, the right to fly that flag and claim its protection, as enjoyed by all regularly documented vessels registered as part of our commercial marine. No state of war existed, conferring upon a maritime power the right to molest and detain upon the high seas a documented vessel, and it can not be pretended that the *Virginius* had placed herself without the pale of law by acts of piracy against the human race. If her papers were irregular or fraudulent, the offense was one against the laws of the United States, justifiable only in their tribunals.

When, therefore, it became known that the *Virginius* had been captured on the high seas by a Spanish man-of-war; that the American flag had been hauled down by the captors; that the vessel had been carried to a Spanish port, and that Spanish tribunals were taking jurisdiction over the persons of those found on her, and exercising that jurisdiction upon American citizens,—not only in violation of international law, but in contravention of the provisions of the treaty of 1795—I directed a demand to be made upon Spain for the restoration of the vessel, and for the return of the survivors to the protection of the United States, for a salute to the flag and for the punishment of the offending parties.

The principles upon which these demands rested could not be seriously questioned, but it was suggested by the Spanish Government that there were grave doubts whether the *Virginius* was entitled to the character given her by her papers, and that therefore it might be proper for the United States, after the surrender of the vessel and the survivors, to dispense with the salute to the flag, should such facts be established to their satisfaction. This seemed to be reasonable and just. I therefore assented to it, on the assurance that Spain would then declare that no insult to the flag of the United States had been intended. I also authorized an agreement to be made that, should it be shown to the satisfaction of this government that the *Virginius* was improperly bearing the flag, proceedings should be instituted in our courts for the punishment of the offense committed against the United States. On her part, Spain undertook to proceed against those who had offended the sovereignty of the United States, or who had violated their treaty rights. The surrender of the vessel and the survivors to the jurisdiction of the tribunals of the United States was an admission of the principles upon which our demand had been founded. I, therefore, had no hesitation in agreeing to the arrangements finally made between the two governments—an arrangement which was moderate and just, and calculated to cement the good relations which have so long existed between Spain and the United States. Under this agreement, the *Virginius*, with the American flag flying, was delivered to the navy of the United States at Bahia Honda, in the Island of Cuba, on the sixteenth. She was in an unseaworthy condition. On the passage to New York, she encountered one of the most tempestuous of our winter storms. At the risk of their lives, the officers and crew placed in charge of her attempted to keep her afloat. Their efforts were unavailing, and she sunk off Cape Fear.

The prisoners who survived the massacres were surrendered at Santiago de Cuba on the eighteenth, and reached the port of New York in safety. The evidence submitted on the part of Spain, to establish the fact that the *Virginius* at the time of her capture was improperly bearing the flag of the United States, is transmitted herewith, together with the opinion of the attorney-general therein, and a copy of the note of the Spanish minister, expressing, on behalf of his government, a disclaimer of any intent of indignity to the flag of the United States.

The opinion of George H. Williams, the Attorney-General, was that the *Virginius* had no right to fly the American flag.

John F. Patterson, registered as owner of the

Virginius, put in a claim to the government, but no attention was ever paid to his demand for damages. Nor were the victims ever requited in any way.

The Cuban revolt flickered on until 1875. Then a truce was had, Spain conceding many reforms, including the abolition of slavery. The country ceased to be a republic, but Don Carlos did not gain the crown. It went to his cousin, Amadeus, and is now worn by the latter's son. But Cuba is free. The memory of the *Virginius* had not died when the *Maine* was blown up, February 15, 1898. Then the people of the United States could stand it no longer, and Spain lost the last of her once great possessions in the western world.

In the diplomatic crossfire that followed the *Virginius* affair, Major-General Daniel E. Sickles, who had tried to be peremptory with Spain, was not upheld by President Grant and resigned his post on December 6, 1873. It was not accepted at the moment, but the general persisted and retired on December twentieth, Caleb Cushing being appointed in his place. It was when Sickles was on his way home that he was drawn into the organization against Jay Gould, as related in a previous chapter.

Besides all this, a minor tragedy fell out of the affair. Ralph Keeler was a brilliant young writer. After ten years as a negro minstrel he had turned man of letters and become the friend of Mark

Twain, Thomas Bailey Aldrich, William Dean Howells and a man respected of Emerson, Longfellow, Lowell and Holmes. He engaged himself as a correspondent of the *New York Tribune* and en route from Havana to Santiago by sea—the only way—disappeared from the ship one night between Havana and Matanzas. Some one knowing his errand must have cast him over the side. It is the only explanation of his disappearance.

That Spain felt no regrets is shown by the fact that Burriel, the butcher, was promoted to a marshal in the army and Castello, Commander of the *Tornado,* to be a colonel of marines.

CHAPTER V

THE TWEED RING

Rise of the Boss to Power in New York City and State—Robbery
and Jobbery—Exposure, Prosecution and Imprisonment—Flight to
Spain—Death in Jail—Fate of Associates.

FOUNDED May 12, 1789, two weeks after
Washington became president, Tammany Hall,
from its vantage in New York, has been ever since
a baleful influence in American politics. William
Mooney, its founder, designed it to be a patriotic
society with the purpose of defending the people
and resisting the inroads of aristocracy. He had
been a soldier in the Revolution, credited, without
proof, with having served on both sides. His creation, the Society of St. Tammany and Columbian
Order, as it was sonorously named, is therefore
the oldest political institution in the country, and
while supporting on the surface the principles of
the Democratic party, has spent most of its long
life in looking out for itself—which means taking
care of the men in control.

It has fathered many scandals, shared in much
pillage and sheltered many rogues, the most eminent and expensive of whom was William Marcy
Tweed, born in Cherry Street, New York, April 3,
1823, who entered politics through the popular

[159]

route of the Volunteer Fire Department, as a member of Americus Hose, and was soon a factor. He served a term in Congress, but found Washington a poor place for pickings, and retired to devote himself to humbler but more profitable place-holding in his native city.

When the Nordics of Scandinavia first established popular government, they met in the open, and, to give speakers a chance to be heard, they stood in a circle, from the center of which the orator had his say. For lack of a better word they called their assemblage a "Thing," which, from its shape, readily became a "ring," representing the ruling power. Tweed transferred the political meaning of "ring" to American politics. He also added "boss" to our political vocabulary. Becoming grand sachem in 1861, he ruled the general committee with such severity as to earn the title which he never tried to discard. To the powers of grand sachem, he added those of deputy street commissioner, a modest office that controlled all the plentiful patronage from contracts to laborers' jobs. To this he annexed, in 1868, the potent position of state senator. A seat in this small body of thirty-two members, gave him the opportunity to control and influence legislation which had much to do with the prosperity of the ring.

The Hall had long had its headquarters at the corner of Frankfort Street and Park Row, in a

THE POWER BEHIND THE THRONE.

HE CANNOT CALL HIS SOUL HIS OWN.

building that later sheltered Charles A. Dana's *Sun* for nearly a half-century. Tweed raised two hundred and fifty thousand dollars and built a new hall on the north side of Fourteenth Street, east of Fourth Avenue, which has since harbored the organization. It received a splendid house-warming on July 4, 1868, when the National Democratic Convention met within its walls to nominate Horatio Seymour and Frank P. Blair, to oppose Lieutenant-General U. S. Grant and Schuyler Colfax on the Republican ticket. John T. Hoffman was next nominated for governor and with Seymour swept the state. Hoffman had occupied the mayor's chair in New York. Tweed managed to have a special election called for the first Tuesday in December, at which A. Oakey Hall was elected mayor by 75,109 votes to 20,835 for Frederick A. Conkling, his Republican opponent. With Hoffman in the governor's chair, Hall in the mayor's office, and Tweed in the State Senate, matters were now prettily adjusted for what was to follow.

According to Tweed's own story, dictated during his confinement as a judgment debtor in Ludlow Street jail, when he was striving for release as a confessed defaulter and was earnestly seeking freedom, the first combination was political, and originated when John T. Hoffman, afterward governor, was mayor of New York. It was composed of Charles G. Cornell, Street Commissioner;

THE DREADFUL DECADE

John T. Hoffman, Mayor; Peter B. Sweeny, Matthew T. Brennan and William M. Tweed. These gentlemen were in the habit of dining together in the City Hall in the keeper's room, and there promised fidelity and devotion to one another. This devotion, as noted above, led Hoffman to the governor's chair, made A. Oakey Hall mayor, and Peter B. Sweeny city chamberlain. Tweed remained content with the humble position of deputy street commissioner, plus his membership in the State Senate. From this vantage point, he opened the door to the city treasury, gingerly at first, by securing, during the session of 1868, the passage of an Act for Adjusting Claims against New York City, which gave to the comptroller, R. B. Connolly, full power to pay such as he pleased and to procure the money by the issue of bonds. This act went into effect on July 1, 1868, and under its provision, Connolly began paying concocted "claims" by interlocking contractors, namely, Andrew J. Garvey, Ingersoll and Company and Keyser and Company. Fifty-five per cent. at first went to the insiders, Tweed getting twenty-five, Connolly twenty and Sweeny ten per cent. of the graft. This process continued for six months, or until January 1, 1869, when the city was mercifully given a breathing spell. In July, 1869, the process was resumed, with an increase from fifty-five to sixty per cent., while on November 1, 1869, the "divvy" rose to sixty-five per cent. of the gross.

THE TWEED RING

Signs of wealth and power now made themselves manifest. Tweed was sought out by men desiring legislation and public privileges. He was seated in directorates of large corporations and was made a director in the company formed to build what became known as the Brooklyn Bridge.* In the chapter on Fisk and Gould his share in the spoliation of the Erie Railroad has been related. His two sons, Richard M. and Charles M., were both in the public crib, one as assistant district attorney and the other as head counsel for the opening of Riverside Drive, a Tweed conception.

Quite naturally, this development bred enemies among the envious in Tammany Hall, who formed a "Young Democracy," to oppose Tweed. These members included Henry W. Genet, also a member of the State Senate, John Morrissey, the pugilist, Thomas J. Creamer, John W. Foley, the gold-pen maker, John Fox, Senator Michael Norton, the "discoverer" of Coney Island, and James O'Brien, who had become sheriff with consequences to Tweed and his coterie.

Before this movement was well under way, a trick devised by Sweeny, whose middle initial was credited with standing for "brains," gave A.

---

*Note: When the financial conditions made it certain that the bridge could not be successfully completed by private means, the directors raised $20,000, which Tweed used to persuade the New York Aldermen to unload one-third of the cost of the structure on New York; Brooklyn, as a city, assuming the other two-thirds.

THE DREADFUL DECADE

Oakey Hall an extended lease of life in the mayor's chair. He had been elected to fill the unexpired term of John T. Hoffman, but claimed a full one. Without notice, in the election of 1869, ballot-boxes were placed at the polls for mayor and tickets given out. The total ballot was 66,619 and of these, Hall received 65,568!

The first aim of the Young Democracy was to put through at Albany a new city charter, giving Home Rule through the Board of Aldermen, and wiping out various commissions. This failed of passage. Tweed captured Henry W. Genet and put through a charter of his own, which left the city helpless in his hands. Connolly had been getting pretty strong. For his sole right to settle claims there was substituted a Board of Audit. It was estimated that it cost one million dollars in bribes to do this. Tweed swore to spending six hundred thousand dollars, and that was by no means all that the thieves in Albany exacted. He paid forty thousand dollars each for the votes of five Republican senators. It was carried in the Senate thirty to two, so thoroughly was the work done, and went through the House one hundred and sixteen to five.

The Young Democracy retired to file their teeth, and Tweed became more powerful, arrogant and grasping than ever before. The Board of Audit included Tweed, Mayor Hall and Connolly. To aid in producing and paying claims, Tweed put through a City and County Tax Levy Bill. Things were now in fine working order, and the dividend rate was raised to eighty-five per cent. Tweed became commissioner of public works under further legislation, and public works were started and pushed in all directions, including a new county court-house in City Hall Park that became the most splendid of all the steals. The election of 1870, for mayor, resulted in a triumph for Hall. He beat the combined Young Democracy and the Republicans, whose candidate was Thomas A. Ledwith, by a vote of 71,037 to 46,692. Of course, there were shameless frauds, although Hoffman, running a second time for governor, ran 15,631 ahead of Hall, and General Stewart L. Woodford, his Republican opponent, got 12,000 more votes than Ledwith. Tweed, himself, was reelected to the Senate and celebrated by giving each alderman one thousand dollars, to be used in supplying the poor with coal. In his own ward, he distributed fifty thousand dollars for relief. This generosity won him great praise, even if Thomas Nast was to use the incident in a stinging cartoon showing Tweed and Sweeny emptying a city safe, with the caption: "Let's blind them with this and then take some more."

The boss must have felt the pressure of the rising reproval. He made a heap of hay in the legislature of 1871, passing for one thing a blanket elevated railroad charter for the Viaduct Railroad, which gave the streets of New York to a concern plus five million dollars in money and an agreement to do all the grading required in its construction at city expense. As directors Tweed put himself, Mayor Hall, Sweeny and Connolly and John J. Bradley in high company, their fellows being Alexander T. Stewart, the great dry-goods merchant, John Jacob Astor, Judge Henry Hilton, August Belmont, John Taylor Johnson, James F. D. Lanier, Franklin Osgood, Charles L. Tiffany, William R. Travers, William Butler Duncan, Levi P. Morton, afterward vice-president of the United States; Hugh Smith, William T. Blodgett, Richard O'Gorman, José F. Navarro, Henry Smith, Edward B. Wesley, Joseph Seligman, Manton Marble and Charles A. Lamont. Incidentally the Viaduct Railway was to be exempt from taxation.

The legislature of 1871 was almost a tie, and when James Irving, a Tammany representative, was expelled for assaulting another member who became eminent, Smith M. Weed, of Plattsburg, Tweed's position grew critical. He held his control by buying up a Republican member, Orange S. Winans. Fisk and Gould assisted in the purchase, which cost Tweed seventy-five thousand dollars and a job from the Erie at the rate of five thousand dollars a year.

The Board of Audit took Sweeny and Genet in as advisers and their ring not only included New York, but Albany. Let Tweed tell his story:

[166]

At these meetings all matters affecting legislation for the city of New York were discussed and bills examined and determined upon to be opposed or supported.

Whenever it was necessary to raise money to pass a bill or affect legislation in any way, A. D. Barber was consulted, and means devised to raise the amount of money which was deemed or found necessary, for that purpose.

Money was raised in the following ways: Mr. Tweed was requested by these gentlemen to act as the cashier, and did so act, the disbursements being generally made by him upon advice or consultation with Barber, who generally took charge of the members of the Assembly, and Mr. Tweed personally of the Senate.

The money was raised by notes of one or more of these gentlemen payable to the order of some one or other of them, and discounted.

These notes were to be, and afterward were, paid by moneys obtained from the city treasury, for which little or no consideration was ever given.

Money was also raised by sending for one or two persons who had business dealings with the city, and notifying them how much money was required from them to pay for legislation; also heads of departments who desired protection or sums of money to be appropriated in the tax levy to be expended by their departments, were notified how much was required from them, with the understanding with them that the money so advanced should be reimbursed to them by payments of bills for which little or no consideration was given to the city.

The said heads of departments made and al-

[167]

lowed such bills to be made up, and approved the same, knowing that they were fraudulent.

For instance, in 1871, the commissioners for building the new court-house desired a large amount—Mr. Tweed thinks one million dollars—inserted in the tax levy of that year. Great opposition was manifested in the legislature to this amount of appropriation, when, by agreement of James H. Ingersoll, one of the court commissioners, with Mr. Tweed, Mr. Tweed was authorized and directed to pay fifteen per cent. of the gross amount which he could secure to be inserted to members of the legislature, and Mr. Ingersoll placed the amount of that percentage, being one hundred and twelve thousand dollars, fifteen per cent. of seven hundred and fifty thousand dollars, which was allowed, in Mr. Tweed's hands, which Mr. Tweed paid to the members of the legislature through A. D. Barber and personally.

This one hundred and twelve thousand dollars, Mr. Tweed learned from Ingersoll, was borrowed by the court-house commissioners—Ingersoll, Coman, Norton and Walsh—from the Tenth National Bank, and is part of the claim of said bank in its present suit against the city.

Money for distribution among members of the ring, Connolly, Sweeny, Hall and Tweed, and their agents, Woodward, Watson, Hugh Smith and James M. Sweeny, and the parties presenting the bills, was raised on fraudulent bills approved by the Board of Audit, the Department of Public Works, or the Comptroller, and paid by the Comptroller, Connolly, out of the moneys of the city.

That these bills were grossly fraudulent in amounts and quantities was well known to all the members of the ring (then Sweeny, Hall, Connolly and Tweed), and were mostly prepared and presented by James Watson or E. A. Woodward, by direction or understanding of the ring or some member of it, in each instance, and distribution of the percentages was made by them.

Mainly, Mr. Tweed and Mr. Connolly had general supervision of everything of this kind, and all complaints, when any one of the ring deemed that his interests were infringed upon, were made to Mr. Tweed.

Nothing was allowed to get away. Printing, always a popular source of graft, was used to great advantage, a company being organized to supply the city with its stationery, *et cetera*. It was called The Manufacturing Stationery Company. An official newspaper, the *Transcript,* was also used as a pocket-filler.

Sweeny's interests in the ring particularly turned toward the selection of candidates to hold judicial positions. Hall was a general adviser and counselor in all legislative and other matters requiring legal skill and ingenuity. Mr. Connolly was the financier, and Mr. Tweed had general charge of all other matters.

Tweed further told of the payment of checks for percentages to various senators and assemblymen, most of them long since dead, and also how the court-house bills were padded by James E. Woodward, or by Cumming B. Tucker, who was superintendent of construction of the court-house.

Woodward was deputy clerk of the Board of Supervisors, and an extra fifteen per cent. was taken out, turned over to Tweed, and by him distributed among the supervisors. Moreover, Tweed told how the famous sheriff, James O'Brien, whose kick over his failure to get all the graft he thought was coming to him really brought down the ring, had an arrangement by which fraudulent bills for stationery, coal, wood and other supplies in the sheriff's office were presented and paid. Then Tweed named one by one Democratic and Republican legislators whom he had given money. John R. Van Pelton, a Republican from Herkimer, got twenty thousand dollars for his vote on the 1869 tax-levy bill, which permitted the excessive New York City appropriations. John F. Hubbard, Jr., a Democrat, got twenty thousand dollars for his vote for the Tweed charter in 1870. Norris Winslow, Republican Senator, was given the two hundred thousand dollars to be distributed among five senators in 1870, when their votes were wanted for the Tweed charter. The senators named by Tweed were William B. Woodin, George Bowen, James Wood, Theodore L. Minier and Winslow himself.

One of the choicest jobs was the Navarro Water-Meter Contract Bill put through the legislature by Alexander Frear. James W. Husted, an eminent Westchester Republican, shared in the glory and profit of this legislation. Says Tweed:

Husted was subsequently a partner with Frear in supplying the Department of Public Works (Tweed's own department) with sand and gravel, for which extortionate sums were paid to them. Mr. Frear acted often for Mr. Tweed in purchasing votes in the Assembly from 1868 to 1871.

Most of the business that Mr. Tweed did in the legislature with senators or assemblymen, where money was needed and used, was done through and by A. D. Barber, who individually saw the members in person and bargained for their votes and times for payment. Large sums of money, banknotes principally, were given Mr. Barber by Mr. Tweed for such purposes from time to time. There was no regular pay for Mr. Barber, or Mr. Abraham Van Vechten, who was associated with him in these transactions, but when the sessions adjourned, they called upon Mr. Tweed and received such compensation as they deemed adequate for their labors.

Barber was a deputy collector of assessments under Tweed, with a fee remuneration which netted him from ten thousand dollars to fifteen thousand dollars a year legitimately.

Tweed touched upon the Navarro scandal. He said:

This legislation, giving the Department of Public Works authority to purchase and use water-meters in the city, was procured by payment of money and promises of place, through Frear, Barber and others. Mr. Tweed's part of the agreement was to obtain the approval of the Navarro meters by the engineers of the Department of Public Works. The test took place, and the engineers decided in favor of the "Navarro." A few days later, at Mr. Sweeny's house, Mr. Sweeny handed Mr. Tweed an agreement or contract with Navarro for the prices of the meter, and Mr. Sweeny said: "It's all right! You have full power and authority to execute it; do so, but first have a direct understanding with Mr. Frear what we are to have out of it!" Mr. Tweed did have an understanding with Mr. Frear that as the bills from time to time were approved and paid by the Comptroller, ten per cent. of the gross amount was to be paid to each member of the ring, Peter B. Sweeny, R. B. Connolly, W. M. Tweed and A. O. Hall, and that no second approval of a bill should be made unless the percentage had been paid on the first, and that the commissions should be paid by Navarro through Mr. Frear.

The Navarro bills ran to stupendous amounts, and Tweed was a large shareholder in the meter company, that being his individual return for getting the bill through in addition to the percentages.

Tweed says further:

The meters themselves were utterly useless, and the price paid far in excess of the value or cost of manufacture.

The confession dealt with the sewer-pipe contracts, on which Tweed got an individual ten per cent. commission, the stationery contracts, in which the same thing occurred, and the Sheriff O'Brien bills for supplies to the county jail, aggregating many hundreds of thousands of dollars, in which the percentages figured again. O'Brien on retiring from office, held a claim for three hundred thousand dollars against the city, a fraudulent one, of course, and Tweed told how he was offered half the claim for one hundred and fifty thousand dollars, and a promise that O'Brien, who had suddenly sided with the reform party, would use his influence to protect Tweed from the impending exposures of the work of the ring. Tweed paid the money, but didn't get the protection. Concerning this he said:

The whole opening of the ring developments arose from the fact that Comptroller Connolly refused to pay this claim of O'Brien.

This is giving O'Brien a credit which he did not deserve, though he wreaked his vengeance in full on Tweed, for whatever reason. The situation had, however, become so brazen that even New York felt disturbed. The city debt had risen from thirty-six million dollars to one hundred and thirty-six million dollars in two years. Taxes grew, and there was an endless assault on real estate for street openings, sewer and water charges. To the intimation that much was wrong, Tweed replied with an examination of Comptroller Connolly's books under the auspices of a most respectable committee composed of Marshall O. Roberts, Moses Taylor, E. D. Brown, of Brown

Brothers, John Jacob Astor, George K. Sistare and Edward Schell. They found all accounts "regular," and commended Connolly for his "honesty" and "faithfulness." How the clever thieves must have laughed in their sleeves!

To add to the éclat, newspapers were subsidized in New York and Albany by liberal "printing" allowances. Tweed edited the columns of Thurlow Weed's *Albany Journal,* that corrupt old lobbyist making about his last killing at this business. Charles A. Dana's *Sun* had been booming the Young Democracy. In March, 1871, it changed its note and actually proposed the erection of a statue of the boss! An association was formed for the purpose of putting the project through, headed by Police Justice Edward J. Shandley. The process of raising funds was stopped by Tweed's declining the honor, as one not to be enjoyed until the end of a man's career. He was rather inclined to suspect sarcasm in the *Sun's* suggestion. The committee, however, was in earnest.

From No. 197 Henry Street on Cherry Hill, in the old Fourth Ward, Tweed now removed to the vicinage of the elect, 41 W. 36th Street. Here his daughter was married with regal splendor. Presents valued at one hundred thousand dollars poured in, which included forty silver services and fifteen articles of jewelry emblazoned with diamonds. The buttons on her shoes were sparklets.

THE TWEED RING

The wedding gown cost four thousand dollars. New York rang with the glory of the event.

Tweed also set up a summer home in Greenwich, Connecticut, since known as the Milbank estate, and installed his political club, called The Americus, after the old engine company, on a point of land projecting into the Sound, the tip of the famous Horse Neck, occupied in later years by the palace of E. C. Benedict. In the adjoining hamlet of Cos Cob, he set up another establishment for a mistress in the guise of a home for his coachman. The stalls for his horses were built of solid mahogany.

It cost one thousand dollars for admittance into the Americus Club, the badge of which was a gold tiger's head with ruby eyes, backed on blue enamel. There were various designs, estimated at two thousand dollars each. From this tiger's head we get the Tammany animal, first developed by Thomas Nast, cartoonist for *Harper's Weekly,* who now began to pencil pitilessly the ring and its leaders. The newspapers were all printing things, and public anxiety became manifest. April 6, 1871, a mass meeting was held in Cooper Union to discuss "the alarming aspects of public affairs generally." William M. Evarts, William Walter Phelps, Judge George C. Barrett and William F. Havemeyer were speakers for the city. Henry Ward Beecher, borrowed from Brooklyn, contributed a burning speech. The growth of the public debt was much dwelt upon, but aside from talk, nothing developed for the moment.

It was left for accident more than design to produce results. James Watson, the slick worker in the Finance Department, had been killed in a sleigh accident in December, 1870, and Stephen C. Lyons, Jr., had taken his place. This promoted Matthew J. O'Rourke, an honest man, to the position of county bookkeeper. He soon became convinced that the books were doctored. Meanwhile, Sheriff James O'Brien, in his pursuit of Tweed, had paid William Copeland, a bookkeeper, to copy the records surreptitiously, and had the copies in his possession. All this while the *Times* was making charges and Nast plying his pitiless pencil. No headway seemed to be made until on a memorable July night O'Brien, seeing that Tweed was likely to weather the storm, took Copeland's copies to the office of the *New York Sun*. Mr. Dana was not there. and he found no editor willing to accept them. Miffed at this, he carried the big bundle across the square to the office of the *Times*. Here he found Louis J. Jennings, the talented Englishman who then edited the paper, and was able to secure attention. The explosion followed. O'Rourke substantiated the figures. In response to a call, a mass meeting was held at Cooper Union on September 4, 1871, presided over by William F. Havemeyer, who had once been mayor. Robert B. Roosevelt and Edwards Pierrepont were among the speakers; Joseph H. Choate presented resolutions calling for action. Seventy men were appointed a committee to deal with the ring. Its members were: Henry G. Stebbins, Edward Solomon, Judge George C. Barrett, Jackson S. Schultz, James Emott, W. H. Neilson, Isaac Bailey, D. Willis James, James M. Brown, Henry Clews, H. F. Spaulding, George W. Lane, W. R. Vermilye, E. Townsend, Lewis Ballard, Paul A. Spofford, James M. Halsted, J. B. Varnum, Robert Hoe, John Wheeler, H. N. Beers, Samuel Christie, Thomas A. Ledwith, Joseph Blumenthal, General John A. Dix, George W. Varian, Joseph J. O'Donough, John M. White, Eugene Ballou, Julius W. Tiemann, Robert W. Howes, W. C. Barrett, Emil Sauer, Albert Klamroth, Frederick Schell, John H. Stewart, Robert L. Kennedy, B. B. Sherman, C. E. Detmold, Charles Creery, Samuel D. Babcock, Edwards Pierrepont, Joseph H. Choate, John Foley, Thomas McLelland, John Straton, Major J. M. Bundy, Henry Nicholl, Dr. E. Krackawitser, Adrian Iselin, Jonathan Sturges, Theodore Steinway, John C. Greene, William W. Wickham, Robert B. Roosevelt, Simon Stern, George Van Slyck, William C. Milloy, Colonel N. G. Dunn, T. C. Cunningham, S. B. Ruggles, Robert B. Nooney, General Francis C. Barlow, Thomas W. Pearsall, William Fliess, Joseph Seligman, Royal Phelps and William Rodde. William F. Havemeyer was chosen chairman.

The advent of the committee was hailed with derision, and as a move by the Republican customhouse ring against a virtuous Democracy, but it was soon seen to be something different. On September seventh, John Foley, of the committee, represented by ex-Judge George C. Barrett, appeared before Tweed's Judge Barnard and asked for a sweeping injunction to restrain tax levies by the Boards of Supervisors and Aldermen, save in obedience to the act passed April 19, 1871, curbing their powers, and including Tweed, Hall, Connolly and Sweeny in its provisions. It also forbade further payment of city moneys by these gentlemen to anybody, with especial reference to the ring supply and printing companies. Barnard granted the injunction as "proper," on the facts as stated.

The next move of the seventy was to appoint a sub-committee to inspect the city vouchers. Monday morning, September 11, 1871, the comptroller announced that his office had been broken into and the vouchers—three thousand, five hundred in number—stolen. This had been done at the instance of Tweed, who employed John C. Heenan, the prize-fighter, then fallen low, William Hennessy Cook, one of his handy men, and one Edward Dunphy, to do the job. They burned the papers in a stove that warmed the room. Edward Haggerty, janitor of the court-house, and Daniel Balch, the watchman, were arrested as a blind and kept some months in the Tombs, never to be tried.

In the midst of the confusions, Mayor Hall maintained a delightful insouciance. He was president of the Lotos Club and was described in the news of the day as presiding with his customary wit and grace, quoting from Homer to prove that Ulysses was founder of the organization. Connolly also kept his poise. His son and close assistant, Townsend Connolly, was tendered the colonelcy of the newly organized Eighty-eighth Regiment, N. G. S. N. Y. Papa Connolly replied for his offspring in his absence abroad, in these touching terms:

"At any moment it would be a matter of great pride to me to see my son in command of a regiment representative of my country, whose flag has floated in the front on every battle-field; but, at this moment, coming from the representatives of a people who are of my race, and who know and appreciate me, the compliment is significant and most grateful. I thank you from the bottom of my heart for it. When my son returns, he will immediately accept the position your confidence has assigned him. Your allusion to my Irish name I am proud of. I am not a man of many words, but I trust I shall leave to my children that name untarnished, to be remembered by all with respect, and perhaps by such as you with a kindlier and tenderer feeling."

In the face of this beautiful sentiment, Mayor Hall now asked Connolly to resign. This the gentleman loftily declined to do, as it might be taken as a confession of guilt. Tweed impudently asked "What are you going to do about it?"—a remark that hastened the vigor of the pursuit. Connolly quietly tried to make terms with the seventy, and after a conference with Chairman W. F. Havemeyer, appointed Andrew H. Green as deputy comptroller—and so completed his own undoing.

Despite the destruction of the vouchers, the sub-committee of the seventy found ample proof of fraud. Garvey had been paid for enough plastering to fill the court-house rooms. The bills for floor coverings would have packed it with carpets. In all, it had cost the city four times its value, or about twelve million dollars, and this was but one item in the Chimborazo of Steal.

The seventy endeavored to indict Mayor Hall. As the panel was packed, Tweed's corrupt judge, George G. Barnard, was forced to dismiss it, but the new lot selected failed to find any excuse for indicting the mayor. He was haled to court but allowed to go without bail.

It had become plain to Samuel J. Tilden, then a distinguished lawyer, who had not been active in politics, that as a Democrat he should seize the situation in the interest of the party, as well as the people. A man of great efficiency, he did not hesitate to step in where others feared to tread, and by doing so he made the fight non-partisan, to his own great subsequent advantage. His coming into the game brought action.

THE TWEED RING

On Thursday, October 19, 1871, Charles O'Conor, the ablest attorney in New York, accepted a retainer as chief council for the prosecution of the ring. He selected as associates, Wheeler H. Peckham, William M. Evarts and ex-Judge James Emott, whose ancestry included one who had been Captain William Kidd's agent in New York some two centuries before. Offices were taken in Brown Brothers building at 59 Wall Street. On October twenty-fifth, the committee fired its first legal gun, in the form of an affidavit signed by Samuel J. Tilden, which read:

City and County of New York, ss.:

Samuel J. Tilden, being duly sworn, deposes and says that, happening casually in the office of the Comptroller of the City of New York, he was consulted by Mr. Andrew H. Green, Deputy Comptroller, and his counsel, as to the notice proposed to be given to the National Broadway Bank in respect to the alleged forgery of the signature of Keyser and Company, as indorsers of certain county warrants; that soon after this, deponent was requested by the said Green to make some investigation in the accounts of the said bank; that deponent noticed on the back of said Keyser warrants pencil memoranda of E. A. W., or E. A. Woodward, which he supposed had been written thereon by the teller who received the deposits, and was led to examine the deposit account of the said Woodward, to see if the Keyser warrants could be identified; that the method of examination adopted was to take a transcript of the de-

[181]

posits as entered on the ledger, and then to decompose the entry of each deposit into the items of which such deposit was made up, by reference to the deposit tickets which had been preserved, and to take a transcript of the debits in the ledger, and then to decompose each entry which was formed of more than one item by reference to the blotter kept by the bank; that deponent traced transactions from the account of the said Woodward into the accounts in the said Bank of Ingersoll and Company, and Andrew J. Garvey, and at last into the account of William M. Tweed, and caused the same process to be applied to each of the said accounts; that the deponent construed the schedule marked E, in the complaint in this action, and wrote every word and figure in the same, except the footings in the several columns; verifying each entry by personal inspection of the transcript made up from the books in the comptroller's office and entries upon the warrants, and with the transcripts from the books of the National Broadway Bank, and from the said deposit tickets, or verifying the same by being called off by George W. Smith and P. W. Rhodes, who assisted the said deponent; that deponent caused the entries purporting to come from the books in the comptroller's office to be compared with the original books of record in said office, and the entries purporting to come from the books of the National Broadway Bank to be compared with transcripts from the entries on the said books, and in both cases the said transcripts with the originals, and believes that each and every entry in the said schedule is correct; that deponent has personally examined the deposit tickets embraced within the period included in the said schedule, left with the deposits of the said Woodward and the said Tweed, mentioned in the said schedule, in connection with Arthur E. Smith, a bookkeeper of the said bank; that this deponent, in examining the tickets of the deposits of the said Woodward, became familiar with the handwriting of the said tickets, and was informed by the said Smith that it was the handwriting of the said Elbert A. Woodward; that deponent noticed, in examining the tickets left with the deposits of the said Tweed, which deposits are contained in the said schedule, that the handwriting of the said tickets accompanying the deposits of the said Tweed is the same handwriting with that of the tickets accompanying the deposits of the said Woodward; and this deponent verily believes that the tickets accompanying the deposits of the said Tweed are in the handwriting of the said Elbert A. Woodward; that deponent also prepared the schedule F, annexed to the complaint; that the summary of the results deduced from the Schedules A and E annexed to the complaint is correct, and truly represents the disposition of the warrants and the collection of their proceeds so far as it purports to represent the same; that deponent caused the statement of the county liabilities, marked Schedule A in the complaint, and No. 1 in the affidavits, to be made, and believes the same to be correct; that deponent has procured a printed copy of certain minutes of the Board of Supervisors, purporting to be issued by Joseph B. Young, clerk of said board, which contains the message of Mayor Hall to the supervisors, under date of August 16, 1871, and apparently delivered to them

August 23, 1871; that copy is annexed hereto and marked No. 3; that deponent has heard read by Charles O'Conor the complaint in this case prepared by him; that as to many of the statements of fact therein contained they are true as to deponent's own knowledge, and that deponent has investigated in respect to all such statements of fact, and is satisfied that they are true.

SAMUEL J. TILDEN.

Accompanying tables showed that one hundred and ninety fraudulent warrants had been issued, under which $6,312,541.37 had been drawn from the city treasury.

The first move under this affidavit was made on Friday, October twenty-eighth, when the following warrant was issued:

Supreme Court—The People of the State of New York vs. William M. Tweed, James H. Ingersoll, Andrew J. Garvey, and Elbert A. Woodward.—By the complaint and affidavit annexed, it appearing that a certain cause of action exists in favor of above-named plaintiffs and against the above-named defendants for deceit and fraud, and that the case is one of those mentioned in Section 179 of the Code, and on motion of the plaintiff's attorney, to wit: the Attorney-General of the State of New York, it is ordered that the Sheriff of the City and County of New York do, and the said sheriff is hereby required forthwith to arrest the defendants above named, William M. Tweed, J. H. Ingersoll, Elbert A. Woodward and A. J. Garvey, and to

hold each of them to bail in the sum of $1,000,000, and to deliver this order to M. B. Champlain, Attorney-General, plaintiff's attorney, at his office, Bureau of Municipal Correction, 51 Wall Street, in the City of New York, on the fourth day of November, A. D. 1871.
Dated October 25, 1871.

W. L. LEARNED,
Justice, Supreme Court.

M. B. Champlain, Attorney-General.
To the Sheriff of the City and County of New York.

This warrant was duly delivered to Tweed's political comrade, Sheriff Matthew T. Brennan, for service. That the document had been issued was soon known and John Graham, Tweed's counsel, came to ask that the sheriff make the arrest as quietly as possible. Tweed's office in the Public Works Department was in the new courthouse. Here the sheriff and one of his clerks, Judson Jarvis, found the great man at one forty-five P. M.

"Mr. Tweed," said Brennan, "I have come on an unpleasant duty." With that he handed the warrant to the boss.

"Yes, gentlemen," he said, "I have been expecting this for some little time. You know that it has been my desire all along to have this matter brought into court, where it can be decided who is right and who is wrong."

Something of a retinue attended the ceremonious arrest. John Graham, W. O. Bartlett and A. J. Vanderpool were there as legal representatives of the boss. Sympathetic friends also present were Jay Gould, Hugh Hastings, the editor of the *New York Commercial Advertiser,* Terence Farley, Benjamin P. Fairchild, Edmund Kelly and Richard M. and Charles M. Tweed, the prisoner's sons. All but the latter were assembled to give bail. Gould qualified in $1,000,000; Fairchild $360,000, Farley $300,000, Kelly $300,000 and Hastings $100,000. Simultaneously the city filed a civil suit against Tweed for $10,000,000, through Corporation Counsel Richard O'Gorman.

Apparently undismayed, Tweed ran again for the Senate and was elected by a majority of nine thousand. Most of the other rogues on the ticket were beaten. Connolly stepped out of office on November twentieth, and Mayor Hall promoted Andrew H. Green to his place. Sweeny had ceased to be city chamberlain and was president of the Park Board. He politely offered to be of service, and not being called for at the moment, departed for Europe. Tweed was indicted for felony on December 16, 1871, and arraigned before Judge Bedford on the sixteenth. The prisoner was remanded to the Tombs without bail, but his attorneys, John Graham, J. E. Burrill, E. W. Stoughton and David Dudley Field, by complaisance of Sheriff Matthew T. Brennan, and escorted by forty policemen, took him before the convenient Judge George G. Barnard, asking for a writ of habeas corpus, under which Barnard released Tweed in five thousand dollars bail. December twenty-ninth, he resigned as commissioner of Public Works, and on the thirtieth, Tammany deposed him as sachem, electing Augustus Schell at a special meeting.

He was not put on trial until January 30, 1873, when the case came up before Judge Noah Davis. The fallen boss was defended by John Graham, David Dudley Field, John E. Burrill, William Fullerton, William O. Bartlett, Willard Bartlett, William Edelsten and Elihu Root, then a budding young barrister who had come from up-state to exercise his adroit mind in the metropolis. The inventory of Tweed's property showed that he had deeded to Mr. Root four lots in Sixtieth Street near Ninth Avenue, then valued at twenty thousand dollars, paying besides two thousand five hundred dollars in cash. Mr. Root was then under thirty. Wheeler H. Peckham, Lyman Tremaine and H. L. Clinton headed the prosecution. The trial lasted the remainder of the month, the jury reporting on January thirty-first that it was unable to agree.

Tweed left the city and spent a season in California, where he might have remained immune. He was advised to stay away but insisted on returning, only to encounter a fresh batch of indictments. He was again placed on trial November 5, 1873, to be defended by the same counsel with

Wheeler H. Peckham prosecuting, and Judge Noah Davis again presiding on the bench.

As the case was called, Tweed's eminent counsel, through John Graham, handed Judge Davis a round-robin protest, holding that he was unfitted to conduct the trial by reason of his presiding at the previous proceeding. Judge Davis regarded this as an attempt at coercion and announced his purpose to deal with it later. The counsel were ordered to proceed.

The jury, after twelve hours' deliberation, not over doubts of guilt, but over items in the count, returned a verdict of "guilty," on Wednesday, November 19, 1873. Sentence was deferred until the Saturday following, November twenty-first, when Judge Davis condemned the dethroned boss to twelve years' imprisonment in the county penitentiary on Blackwell's Island, and to pay a fine of $12,750.18. In form, the sentence of imprisonment was divided into twelve one-year sentences on as many different counts. He had been convicted on one hundred and two.

Tweed remained in the office of Sheriff Matthew T. Brennan until midnight, awaiting the outcome of some legal move that would save him from a cell. Nothing eventuated. He was therefore taken to the Tombs and locked up—a convict at last. He remained in the Tombs until Saturday, November twenty-ninth, when at the peremptory order of Attorney-General Francis C.

Barlow, he was taken to Blackwell's Island. The day before, James H. Ingersoll and John D. Farrington were sentenced to five years and eighteen months, respectively, in Sing Sing for forgeries committed in the interest of the ring. Also Judge Davis fined Messrs. John Graham, W. O. Bartlett and William Fullerton two hundred fifty dollars each for contempt of court, committed when as Tweed's counsel they signed and presented the protest against his again sitting in the case. Elihu Root and William Edelsten, being young, were let off with a reprimand.

Tweed's family accompanied him to the island, where it took some time to array him in prison garb, as among the striped "hand-me-downs" it was hard to find a pair of trousers wide enough to fit the bulky ex-boss. The cold bath taken under regulations gave him a chill, which sent him forthwith to the comfortable hospital, where he was to spend most of the single year the law kept him confined. When his pedigree was taken at the prison office he gave his occupation as "statesman," and professed to have no religious belief.

Tweed's attorneys appealed the sentence on the ground that under the statute no one could be sent for more than one year in the county prison, and that, while Judge Davis had made the twelve-year detention in periods of continuing twelve-months, it was illegal. The Court of Appeals so held, and Tweed was released from duress January 15, 1875.

As no restitution had been made, Samuel J. Tilden caused the passage of an act by the legislature which would permit civil actions for recovery. This statute was now invoked and Tweed arrested. Bail was fixed at three million dollars, which was not forthcoming, and he was committed to Ludlow Street jail, with many privileges, not the least of which was going about town in the custody of a couple of keepers. December 4, 1875, he made a visit to his house and failed to reappear. The hue and cry that followed did not produce a very diligent search. He had left his house by the roof and, going to the scuttle of a mansion at the end of the row, descended to the street. Having changed his clothes and removed his beard, he then took an evening train on the New Haven Road to Cos Cob. This station was one at which all trains stopped, to make certain that the single-track bridge over the wide estuary of the Mianus River, was clear. Henry B. Marshall, the night telegraph operator, recognized Tweed, but did not give the alarm. Marshall retired from railroading soon after and became a prosperous business man in Greenwich.

Tweed was taken to the house in a secluded section of Cos Cob, where a few years earlier he had installed his mistress. Here he remained hidden until the tumult died down. Through arrangements made with the captain of a sailing schooner, he departed for Florida and thence made his way to Cuba. He was recognized and arrested in

A Group of Vultures waiting for the Storm to
"Blow Over"—"Let us *Prey*"

Havana, but the use of money set him free to sail in the Spanish bark *Carmen* for Vigo, Spain. One of Thomas Nast's pictures, *Tweedle-dum and Tweedle-dee,* had preceded him. It showed the boss dragging two shrinking figures of children. The tender-hearted offspring of the Inquisition concluded he was a child stealer in spite of his benevolent features, and put him under arrest as an abductor. Although the United States had no extradition treaty with Spain, thanks to the amiability of Secretary of State Hamilton Fish, in the *Virginius* affair, the Spanish authorities were pleased to honor a requisition with promptness.

With the dignity befitting his exploits, the U. S. S. *Franklin,* which had been Admiral D. G. Farragut's last flagship, and then the finest vessel in the navy, was sent to bear the boss home. He was landed in New York, November 23, 1876. Coming over he messed with the captain, played cribbage in the ward-room, and was guarded on deck by a respectful marine.

During his absence the city had secured a judgment by default against Tweed of six million dollars. By transfer to his son, Richard M. Tweed, previous to his trial, he had disposed of about two million, four hundred thousand dollars in real estate. He testified that he had never been worth more than three million dollars. Where then went the vast stealings? Bribes and "divvies" took, perhaps, the greater part, but it is reasonably sure that his Wall Street friends must have taken much of it, following their custom of luring the pay granted for public favors back into their own pockets. His escape, he said, had cost sixty thousand dollars and his lawyers four hundred thousand dollars. He was also six hundred thousand dollars out from a bad investment in the Metropolitan Hotel, purchased for his son.

Much money also lay sunk in uncompleted undertakings. For years a forest of iron stood at the corner of Fifty-ninth Street and Fifth Avenue, representing the frame work of a fine hotel to have been financed by Tweed. It finally became the Hotel Savoy. A boulevard on the heights back of Piermont on the Hudson, designed to open a large amount of real estate, also served as a plantation for underbrush.

As a judgment-debtor, Tweed remained in Ludlow Street jail, paying seventy-five dollars a week for the warden's parlor. His health suffered from the confinement and the reaction of his hard-lived life. April 12, 1878, saw his end.

To S. Foster Dewey, his secretary, he made his last remark: "I have tried to right some great wrongs. I have been forbearing with those who did not deserve it. I forgive all who have ever done evil to me, and I want all those whom I have harmed to forgive me."

Luke, his faithful black attendant, held his hand when he died. His demise attracted little attention, and but eight carriages followed his body to the grave. It was interred in Woodlawn. Pneumonia was the immediate cause of death.

So ended an amazing career.

Physically, Tweed is described as having been five feet, ten inches in height, broad-shouldered and heavily built. At the time of his fall much of his sandy hair had disappeared, and his beard was almost gray. His eyes were gray and his nose, thick and long, gave his face the look of a vulture, a characteristic which Thomas Nast made the most of. His forehead was that of an intellectual man, broad and high. He was sententious in speech and forceful in manner, never lacking decision or purpose. His abilities, honestly exercised, could have easily carried him far.

As for the rest of the rogues, Monday afternoon, November 24, 1871, Henry W. Genet was arrested as a member of the ring, charged with the larceny of lumber from the Harlem court-house, which he had used to build him a fine home at the corner of Fifth Avenue and One-hundred-twenty-sixth Street; also for certifying that a bill of J. McB. Davidson for $4,802, for work on the court-house, was correct. He was released under $2,000 bail on each charge, tried and found guilty on Friday, December 19, 1873. He was remanded in custody of the sheriff for sentence on the following Monday, but vanished.

Genet came of notable ancestry. He was a

grandson of Citizen Edmond Charles Genet, Minister to the United States from France at the age of nineteen, who made himself so offensive to President George Washington that his recall was demanded in 1793. That was a year when heads were not safe in Paris, so he chose to remain in America. He married a daughter of Governor George Clinton. President Washington refused to honor extradition papers from the Jacobin Government of France. Henry W. Genet kept in hiding until February 4, 1878, when he appeared before Judge Daniels and gave twenty-five thousand dollars bail pending an appeal from the conviction. The Court of Appeals took its time about the matter. The decision was adverse when it came, and Judge Daniels sentenced Genet to eight months on Blackwell's Island, March 12, 1881. This prison term was served. He died, September 6, 1889, aged sixty-one.

Of Tweed's other companions, "Slippery Dick" Connolly made the cleanest "get-away." In the first suit brought, his brother Charles, who had shared with him in his pickings, put up five hundred thousand dollars in bail, after it had been reduced from one million dollars, which was forfeited, and the pair departed for France, never to return. Connolly was also under fifteen indictments, and Judge Barnard had accepted fifteen thousand dollars bail. Both were reported to have died in Marseilles in poor circumstances, in 1880.

Connolly had insured much of his gains against capture by making his New York property over to his two daughters, Mrs. Joel Adam Fithian and Mrs. Robert L. Hutchings, the latter's husband being surrogate at the time. In all he was supposed to have sequestrated about six million dollars. The two ladies always lived in affluence and took on important acquaintances in New York and Paris, where they resided after the flight in 1872.

The Fithians appear to have absorbed most of the money. J. Adam Fithian had kept a small tobacco store on Canal Street. In exile, he had a mansion near the Parc Monceaux, a château on Lake Geneva, and a yacht on its waters. A daughter became the Countess de Gabriac.

One of the good stories of the day concerned a fine house that Charles Connolly built for himself at One-hundred-eighty-first Street and the Hudson River. Richard B. and Tweed, driving up to take a look at the new structure, found a workman setting up a statue.

"Who the h—l is that?" asked Tweed.

"That's Mercury, the God of Merchants and Thieves," replied the toiler.

"Bully," said Connolly. "Put him over the front door."

Peter B. Sweeny, who also departed for the gaieties of Paris, came back in 1877, with a proposition to compromise and be let alone. The aldermen made an investigation that led nowhere,

but Sweeny settled on account of the estate of his
dead brother, James M., paying back four hundred
thousand dollars. He claimed that he had even
declined the honest graft enjoyed by his predeces-
sors in the office of city chamberlain. Thereafter he was not troubled, but lived as he liked,
abroad and at home. On Monday, September 24,
1894, he filled the entire first page of Charles A.
Dana's *New York Sun* with a review of the Rapid
Transit Act, upon which the city's subways came
to be built in a decade or so. He was "thick in"
with Jake Sharp, the Broadway franchise briber,
and naturally out of sympathy with honest meth-
ods. John J. Bradley, his brother-in-law, was also
a contractor much favored by the Ryan-Whitney
combination. He brazenly argued that the old
New York City Railway Charter, granted Alexander T. Stewart, John Jacob Astor, August
Belmont, Henry Hilton and William Butler
Duncan, was still in force. This was Tweed's celebrated "viaduct" scheme. Duncan's close relations
to Charles A. Dana explain the prominence given
the worthless claim by the *Sun.*

The article naturally provoked comment, in
which the *World* was especially severe. Sweeny
replied to it in a letter in which he averred: "I had
no complicity in the ring frauds. When I went to
Europe, it was after investigation and after all
imputations against me had been withdrawn or dismissed. My intended departure was heralded in

all the newspapers. When the charges were revived for political reasons, I returned voluntarily to meet them and was exonerated in open court. At the time of my departure, I did not hold the office of city chamberlain, but that of president of the Department of Parks. This department came through the fire unscathed." This may have been because Henry Hilton and Andrew H. Greene were his associates.

Sweeny also appeared in print again on January 14, 1899, with an open letter to Governor Theodore Roosevelt, in which he objected to abolishing the office of city chamberlain, recommended in Roosevelt's first message to the legislature.

He died at Lake Mahopac, New York, August 31, 1911, at the home of his son, Assistant Corporation Counsel Arthur Sweeny, from the after effects of a fall, in the eighty-sixth year of his life.

Andrew J. Garvey, the prolific plasterer, who turned state's evidence, also went abroad with his spoil. He died at Southampton, England, April 5, 1897, leaving an estate of five hundred thousand dollars, of which two hundred thousand dollars was given to New York charities. He had changed his name to A. Jeffries Garvie and lived as a gentleman on his pickings. Like Tweed, he was buried in Woodlawn.

Mayor Hall was finally put on trial for "wilful" neglect of duty. That he had been neglectful went without saying. To prove it was another matter. The case came to trial on December 22, 1873. Hall appeared for himself, with his partner, A. J. Vanderpool. No evidence was put in by the defense which rested on the plea of not guilty. The jury acquitted him on the twenty-sixth after a four-hour session. He served out his term and was succeeded by William F. Havemeyer, who won a three-cornered fight in the election of 1872, against Abram R. Lawrence, the Tammany candidate, and ex-Sheriff James O'Brien, the avenger, running on his own hook.

Three judges had soiled their ermine to serve Tweed—Albert Cardozo, John H. McCunn and George G. Barnard. Facing impeachment, Cardozo resigned. McCunn and Barnard were impeached and removed from the bench. After the latter's death one million dollars in cash and bonds were found among his effects.

The extent of all the stealings was never exactly totaled. Matthew J. O'Rourke fixed the figure at seventy-five million dollars. Only eight hundred seventy-six thousand dollars was recovered from the ring.

The late Joseph Howard, Jr., a journalist of easy fortune, once related this adventure with Sweeny and Tweed:

"Brick" Pomeroy had transplanted his *Lacrosse Democrat* to New York. Howard was managing editor, and the sheet was needy. One day the pair called, and introducing themselves, suggested that the *Democrat* should become a "corporation" newspaper, lifting reports of council proceedings from the official *Evening Express,* owned by James and Erastus Brooks, and charging at the rate of thirty cents per agate line, though setting the matter in the larger size called nonpareil. Howard wanted to know what it would be worth in the aggregate.

"That depends," replied Tweed. "I chould think it would be a very handsome addition to the income of a newly started paper, and all we want in return is that you will look out for us."

Howard agreed. When the bill against the city mounted to five thousand eight hundred dollars, there was a call for the money. Going to the comptroller's office, the collector was turned over to a clerk who, in adjournment to Delmonico's, said that he would put the bill through at a discount of twenty per cent. To this the *Democrat* demurred. Howard saw Tweed, who treated it as a great joke and sent this command to Connolly:

"Dear Dick: For God's sake pay ——'s bill. He tells me your people ask 20 per cent. The whole d——d thing isn't but $1,100. If you don't pay it I will. Thine, William M. Tweed."

The bearer of the note could not find Connolly, and his deputy was unmoved. So Howard went to Sweeny. He put it through without the discount.

CHAPTER VI

BEECHER AND TILTON

The Great Brooklyn Scandal—Victoria C. Woodhull and Tennessee
Claflin—Plymouth Pastor Sued for One Hundred Thousand Dollars—Jury Disagrees after a Six-Months Trial—An Era of Super-
emotion.

BROOKLYN, in the 'sixties, and for twenty years
or more later, was rather remarkable for its
churches, numerically speaking, and for an unusual
number of able preachers, the greatest of whom
was Henry Ward Beecher, pastor of Plymouth, a
Congregational congregation. Sharing his repute
were the Reverend T. DeWitt Talmage, a pirouett-
ing Presbyterian, the Reverend Doctor Richard
S. Storrs, head of the Congregational Church of
the Pilgrims, Theodore L. Cuyler, Doctor William
Ives Buddington, Henry Martyn Scudder and
John White Chadwick, a celebrated Unitarian.
Beecher and Talmage were most in the public eye.
Their churches were easily located on Sunday by
the crowds marching toward them. Talmage was
an ultra-sensational exhorter, who excited his
hearers, but Mr. Beecher had the faculty of reaching deep emotions. He was not only the foremost
preacher in America, perhaps in the world, but a
factor in political affairs. He had been a vigorous

leader in the anti-slavery cause, a Republican of
eminence, who ranked with Horace Greeley and
Charles Sumner, and in all ways was a conspicuous
citizen of the community in which he lived.

Moreover, his writings had such vogue that
they established the prosperity of a semi-religious
journal, the *Independent,* published in New York
by Henry C. Bowen, one of Mr. Beecher's parish-
ioners, who also owned the *Brooklyn Union.*
Beecher and Bowen parted company, the former
to become editor of the *Christian Union,* published by J. B. Ford and Company, leaving the
Independent in charge of a brilliant youth named
Theodore Tilton, who had been a protégé of
Beecher and an ardent follower of his preaching
at Plymouth. Tilton was married. His wife,
Elizabeth, was a shy, sentimental woman who took
no part in her husband's public career, but was
also an attendant at Plymouth and, as asserted by
Mr. Beecher, a friend of his wife and himself
mainly through their interest in the brilliant Theodore.

The *Christian Union,* cutting into the circulation of the *Independent,* caused a coolness between
Beecher and Bowen, who felt that Tilton did not
fill the bill as well as he might and transferred him
to the editorship of the *Brooklyn Union* at five
thousand a year under a five-year contract, with a
bonus for special service to the *Independent.*
Tilton was then (1870) thirty-five years old and

had gained a ranking position for himself in journalism. He had not quarreled with Mr. Beecher, but he was soon to fall into evil company and so deeply to tarnish his name that he sought to rub the verdigris off on the good repute of his pastor. Conveniently, Bowen hoped to disparage Beecher so as to break the growth of the *Christian Union.* Mr. Beecher was apparently invincible. His church overflowed with auditors. He was in nationwide demand as a lecturer. A novel, *Norwood,* published in Robert Bonner's *New York Ledger,* had been an enormous success, and he had undertaken to write a *Life of Christ* that bade fair to break the record as a best seller. His publishers counted heavily upon it. The reception given the first volume quite justified their hopes. Before the second could be produced something happened that, in the words of Samuel Wilkeson, "knocked the *Life of Christ* higher than a kite."

That Tilton had become indifferent to the plain little wife who could not shine with him, there is no doubt. Neither is there any question that she sought consolation from her distinguished pastor, the exact extent of which was never proved. In December, 1870, upon Mr. Beecher's return from an extended lecture tour, Mrs. Tilton, through Bessie Turner, a very astute young girl, who had been living in the Tilton household, sent word to Mr. Beecher that she was in deep trouble and wished his advice. The girl told Mr. Beecher,

according to his account, a story of cruelty and
abuse endured from Theodore by the meek Elizabeth, who had left her own fireside and gone to her
mother. Inexpressibly shocked, Mr. Beecher says
in his memorandum written to cover the affair:
"I immediately visited Mrs. Tilton at her mother's
and received an account of her home life, and of
the despotism of her husband, and of the management of a woman he had made housekeeper, which
seemed like a nightmare dream. The question was,
should she go back, or separate forever from her
husband." He did not advise her at the moment,
but asked permission to call again with Mrs.
Beecher for further conference, as her judgment
"in all domestic relations, I thought better than my
own."

Mrs. Beecher, after hearing Mrs. Tilton's
story, "was extremely indignant toward Mr. Tilton," and declared that "no consideration on earth
would induce her to remain an hour with a man
who had treated her with a hundredth part of such
insult and cruelty."

Feeling, he adds, as strongly on the subject as
did Mrs. Beecher, he yet hesitated to convey a
conclusion, so it was agreed that Mrs. Beecher
should call again and deliver final judgment. The
next day, when Mrs. Beecher was about to depart
for the visit, "there was company, and the children
were present," which forbade exchange of words
on the delicate topic, so Mr. Beecher wrote on a

scrap of paper what proved to be a most imprudent note, reading: "I incline to think your view is right, and that a settlement of support will be wisest, and that in his present desperate state her presence near him is far more likely to produce hatred than her absence."

This opinion was duly delivered by Mrs. Beecher. Beecher adds parenthetically: "Mrs. Tilton did not tell me that my presence had anything to do with this trouble, nor did she let me know that on the July previous he (Mr. Tilton) had extorted from her a confession of excessive affection for me."

What came next Mr. Beecher and his supporters always held was the outcome of a conspiracy between Henry C. Bowen and Tilton to break the progress of the *Christian Union,* by driving him from Plymouth pulpit. On the evening of December 27, 1870, in the midst of the Merry Yuletide, Mr. Bowen called at the Beecher residence, Brooklyn, and delivered this demand in writing:

"Henry Ward Beecher: For reasons which you explicitly know, and which I forbear to state, I demand that you withdraw from the pulpit and quit Brooklyn as a residence.
Theodore Tilton."

"I read it over twice," records the recipient, turned to Bowen and said: "This man is crazy; this is sheer insanity," and other like words.

[204]

Bowen pretended not to have known the contents of the note, and, according to Mr. Beecher, went into a long detail of his troubles with Tilton, whose "social and religious views" had compelled him to reduce him from editor to contributor on the *Independent*. Whatever there was of conspiracy, seems to have disappeared for the moment. Mr. Bowen and Mr. Beecher parted in apparent accord of opinion, that Theodore Tilton had become an undesirable. As the ruse had not scared Beecher from his pulpit, Bowen promptly dismissed Tilton from his employ on both the *Union* and the *Independent*. Mr. Beecher declared that in the course of their quarrel, Bowen had told Tilton of his (Beecher's) comments on his character. The Beecher narrative continues: "It now appears that on the thirtieth of December, 1870, Mr. Tilton, having learned that I had replied to his threatening letter by expressing such an opinion of him as to set Mr. Bowen finally against him, and bring him face to face with immediate ruin, extorted from his wife, then suffering under a severe illness, a document incriminating me, and prepared an elaborate attack upon me."

In saying this, Mr. Beecher overlooks certain preliminaries. The note of demand upon Mr. Beecher to remove himself from church and Brooklyn, was based upon a confession of intimacy between Beecher and Mrs. Tilton, made by her some weeks before. When Tilton was dismissed by

[205]

Bowen, who, in so doing, broke a contract, he took on as his attorney, Francis D. Moulton, a member of the Plymouth congregation, who figures thereafter as a "mutual friend." He brought Beecher and Tilton into a conference, and smoothly intimated that the former and Bowen were conspiring to destroy Tilton, insisting that Beecher's belief in Tilton's baseness was all founded on misinformation, so oiling the tracks to bring the injured parties together. "The case, as it then appeared to my eyes," wrote Mr. Beecher, "was strongly against me." He could not see how he could defend himself save by pouring indignation on Mrs. Tilton, and holding her up to contempt for having "thrust her affection upon me unsought." In this mood he disclaimed all intent to harm Tilton in his home or his business, and "with inexplicable sorrow I both blamed and defended Mrs. Tilton in one breath." The wily Moulton led him only deeper into the mess, tempting him to salve the wounds of Theodore, and to urge Elizabeth to have confidence in a "mutual friend," who was all the time playing double. "My age and experience in the world," wrote Mr. Beecher in his bitter afterreflections, "should have put me more on my guard." Unfortunately for him, they did not.

His first false step was to go with Moulton, on December thirtieth, to call on Mrs. Tilton and exact from her the following absolution:

BEECHER AND TILTON

December 30, 1870.
Wearied with importunity and weakened by sickness, I gave a letter implicating my friend, Henry Ward Beecher, under the assurances that that would remove all difficulties between me and my husband. That letter I now revoke. I was persuaded to it—almost forced—when I was in a weakened state of mind. I regret it, and recall all its statements.   E. R. Tilton.

Tilton was, of course, at once advised of the happening and promptly secured recantation in this form:

December 30, 1870—Midnight.
My dear Husband: I desire to leave with you, before going to bed, a statement that Mr. Henry Ward Beecher called on me this evening, and asked me if I would defend him against any accusation in a Council of Ministers; and I replied solemnly, that I would, in case the accuser was any other person than my husband. He (H. W. B.) dictated a letter, which I copied as my own, to be used by me as against any other accuser except my husband. This letter was designed to vindicate Mr. Beecher against all other persons save only yourself. I was ready to give him this letter because he said with pain that my letter in your hands addressed to him, dated December twenty-ninth,"had struck him dead, and ended his usefulness." You and I are pledged to do our best to avoid publicity.

God grant a speedy end to all further anxieties.   Affectionately,
Elizabeth.

Coincidentally, Mr. Beecher placed himself at the mercy of Tilton and Moulton by giving the latter the following document, "in confidence,"— to a confidence man:

Brooklyn, January 1, 1871.
[In trust with F. D. Moulton.]

My dear Friend Moulton: I ask through you, Theodore Tilton's forgiveness, and I humble myself before him as I do before my God. He would have been a better man in my circumstances than I have been. I can ask nothing except that he will remember all the other hearts that would ache. I will not plead for myself. I must even wish that I were dead. But others must live and suffer. I will die before any one but myself shall be inculpated. All my thoughts are running toward my friends, toward the poor child lying there and praying with her folded hands. She is guiltless, sinned against, bearing the transgression of another. Her forgiveness I have. I humbly pray to God that He may put it into the heart of her husband to forgive me.

I have trusted this to Moulton in confidence.

H. W. Beecher.

Then on February 7, 1871, he wrote Mrs. Tilton a letter, designed, he says, to give her the desired confidence in Moulton, but between the lines it would seem more like a plea for help for himself. He again set forth that he was not long for this world—though he survived sixteen years. "I alluded to the fact," he says, "that when I saw her last I did not expect to be alive many days." It is a wonder that, with his full habit, he did not collapse under the strain, which went on under the surface for months, with plenty of whispering to keep it alive, but no public exposure of the strife.

Upon quitting Bowen, Tilton established the *Golden Age,* a literary weekly with much merit, to which he contributed an interesting serial, *Tempest Tossed,* and for the first time brought the Sargasso Sea into fiction. The *Golden Age* was not golden in receipts; he had a struggle to get on, and must have more than once looked back to the fat "flesh pots" of Brother Bowen. Both the *Brooklyn Union* and the *Independent* were very profitable. Bowen deftly combined the growing business of life insurance with piety in the *Independent,* and the page advertisements of the corporations added to his affluence. Hard pressed, Tilton now resorted to blackmail, preparing and putting into type of the *Golden Age* an article in which he neatly charged Bowen with making accusations of a scandalous nature against Beecher. Moulton took a proof of this to Beecher in February, 1872, graciously saying that while it let the cat out of the bag, it was an attack on Bowen, not Beecher. The latter, in great alarm, got together with Bowen, and as a condition of non-publication, Bowen settled with Tilton for seven thousand dollars, while the trio signed an agreement of "amnesty, concord and future peace." It read:

We three men, earnestly desiring to remove all causes of offense existing between us, real or fancied, and to make Christian reparation for injuries done, or supposed to have been done, and to efface the disturbed past, and to provide concord, goodwill, and love for the future, do declare and covenant each to the others as follows:

I. I, Henry C. Bowen, having given credit, perhaps without due consideration, to tales and innuendoes affecting Henry Ward Beecher, and being influenced by them, as was natural to a man who receives impressions suddenly, to the extent of repeating them (guardedly, however, and within limitations, and not for the purpose of injuring him, but strictly in the confidence of consultation), now feel therein that I did him wrong.

Therefore, I disavow all the charges and imputations that have been attributed to me, as having been by me made against Henry Ward Beecher, and I declare fully and without reserve that I know nothing which should prevent me from extending to him my most cordial friendship, confidence, and Christian fellowship; and I expressly withdraw all the charges, imputations, and innuendoes imputed as having been made and uttered by me and set forth in a letter written to me by Theodore Tilton on the first day of January, 1871; and I sincerely regret having made any imputations, charges, or innuendoes unfavorable to the Christian character of Mr. Beecher, and I covenant and promise that for all future time I will never by word or deed recur to, repeat, or allude to any or either of said charges, imputations, and innuendoes.

II. And I, Theodore Tilton, do, of my own

free will and friendly spirit toward Henry C. Bowen and Henry Ward Beecher, hereby covenant and agree that I will never again repeat, by word of mouth or otherwise, any of the allegations, or imputations, or innuendoes contained in my letter hereunto annexed, or any other injurious imputations or allegations suggested by or growing out of these; and that I will never again bring up or hint at any cause of difference or ground of complaint heretofore existing between the said Henry C. Bowen and myself or the said Henry Ward Beecher.

III.   And I, Henry Ward Beecher, put the past forever out of sight and out of memory.   I deeply regret the causes of suspicion, jealousy, and estrangement which have come between us.   It is a joy to me to have my old regard for Henry C. Bowen and Theodore Tilton restored, and a happiness to me to resume the old relations of love, respect, and reliance to each and both of them.   If I have said anything injurious to the reputations of either, or have detracted from their standing and fame as Christian gentlemen and members of my church, I revoke it all, and heartily covenant to repair and reinstate them to the extent of my power.

HENRY WARD BEECHER.
THEODORE TILTON.
HENRY C. BOWEN.

The article did not appear in the *Golden Age* as the result of this treaty.

A new element now came into the commotion. America never produced two more extraordinary women than Victoria Claflin and her sister, Tennessee. They were daughters of Reuben Buckman Claflin, a native of Stansfield, Massachusetts, and his wife, Rosanna. Claflin was a country lawyer who settled at Homer, Ohio, where the two notables were born, Victoria, September 3, 1838, and Tennessee, October 26, 1845. When fourteen Victoria married a doctor, Canning Woodhull, and remained his wife fourteen years; then divorce parted them. The two sisters now started on their adventures, in 1863 turning up at Ottawa, Illinois, where they took over an old hotel, the Fox House, and set up a cure-all sanitarium, the treatment at which was based on several varieties of the plentiful "isms" of the day, including spiritualism. Victoria, being the older, was the master mind. Some failure at conquering cancer with a mustard plaster broke up the enterprise, and the pair set themselves up for a time in Cincinnati, where the whisky kings of the ring days paid tribute to their beauty. The breaking up of this illicit industry caused the young women to seek a new field in New York. Here they arrived during the speculative fever engendered by Fisk and Gould and the Drew-Vanderbilt conflicts, setting up a brokerage shop at 44 Broad Street, where it is to be suspected they sold much more than railroad shares. They contrived to create the impression that Commodore Vanderbilt was behind them, and while it is doubtful if the brokerage business was ever large, they claimed great profits in Erie and caused a deal of commotion.

Though New York was then a most immoral town, the limitations on women were severe. They were not allowed to enter public places of entertainment or restaurants without escort. Prudishness repressed the respectable, while the wanton flourished. The movement for equal suffrage that rose with the adoption of the Fourteenth Amendment was being actively agitated by Susan B. Anthony, Elizabeth Cady Stanton and their few followers. They were treated with scorn by the political leaders of the day, and faced arrest and many cruel affronts. To this cause the two bold sisters addressed themselves, establishing *Woodhull and Claflin's Weekly* with their Wall-Street gains. It not only advocated equal rights at the polls, but in everything else, including matrimony, or love life without it. The restrictions against lone women in public places were fought and made ridiculous. When refused service at Delmonico's, Tennessee brought her cab driver in as escort. Then Charles Delmonico ordered the soup served. She commandeered a Gilsey House porter to secure a seat to see Madame Ristori. Being young and attractive, she went about securing subscriptions for the *Weekly* among prominent business men with incidental success, while Victoria spoke from the platform to crowded houses. The latter was an orator of unusual gifts and pleasing presence, coming nearer the masculine ideal of a good speaker than either Anna E. Dickinson or Mrs. Mary A. Livermore, both eminent contemporaries. She was well-enough thought of on February 11, 1871, to present the views of the Women's Rights Association at a hearing before the House Judiciary Committee held in Washington. Susan B. Anthony, Elizabeth Cady Stanton, Pauline Wright Davis, and others, as well as Sister Tennessee, kept her company. She made an impressive argument and was listened to respectfully by the hard-boiled members of the committee, one of whom was Benjamin F. Butler.

In the process of proclaiming freedom for their sex, the sisters took to printing the scandals of double life that were plentiful enough in New York at the time. They declared for the single standard and saw no reason why women should be condemned for ways for which men went unscathed. The *Weekly* requiring a managing editor, the ladies engaged Captain J. H. Blood, late of the Sixth Missouri Regiment, to assist. Subsequently, Victoria took him on as a husband, Doctor Woodhull having been dropped officially. Colonel Blood moved into the elegant ménage maintained by the sisters at 44 West Thirty-eighth Street, one of the first consequences of which was the expulsion of their aged mother, who, averring that Blood had threatened her life, haled him into court on May 15, 1871. The old lady declared

that both husbands of her daughter Victoria had
been kept in the house at once, a statement that
naturally evoked comment concerning one living
in a glass house who threw stones. This Mrs.
Woodhull answered in a "card," published in the
World of May twenty-second:

To the Editor of The World:
Sir: Because I am a woman, and because I
conscientiously hold opinions somewhat different
from the self-elected orthodoxy which men find
their profit in supporting, and because I think it
my bounden duty and my absolute right to put forward my opinions and to advocate them with my
whole strength, self-orthodoxy assails me, vilifies
me, and endeavors to cover my life with ridicule
and dishonor.

This has been particularly the case in reference
to certain law proceedings into which I was re-
cently drawn by the weakness of one very near
relative and the profligate selfishness of other
relatives.

One of the charges against me is that I lived
in the same house with my former husband, Doctor Woodhull, and my present husband, Captain
Blood.

The fact is a fact. Doctor Woodhull, being
sick, ailing, and incapable of self-support, I felt it
my duty to myself and to human nature that he
should be cared for, although his incapacity was in
no wise attributable to me. My present husband,
Captain Blood, not only approved of this charity,
but cooperates in it. I esteem it one of the most
virtuous acts of my life; but various editors have

stigmatized me as a living example of immorality and unchastity.

My opinions and principles are subjects of just criticism. I put myself before the public voluntarily. I know full well that the public will criticize me and my motives and actions in their own way and at their own time. I accept the position. I except to no fair analysis and examination, even if the scalpel be a little merciless.

But let him who is without sin cast the stone. I do not intend to be made the scapegoat of sacrifice to be offered up as a victim to society by those who cover over the foulness of their lives and the feculence of their thoughts with a hypocritical mantle of fair professions, and by diverting public attention from their own iniquity in pointing the finger at me.

I know that many of my self-appointed judges and critics are deeply tainted with the vices they condemn; I live in the house with one who was my husband; I live as wife with one who is my husband; I believe in Spiritualism; I advocate Free Love in its highest, purest sense, as the only cure for the immorality, the deep damnation by which men corrupt and disfigure God's most holy institution of sexual relation. My judges preach against free love openly, practise it secretly; their outward seeming is fair, inwardly they are full of "dead men's bones and all manner of uncleanliness." For example, I know of one man, a public teacher of eminence, who lives in concubinage with the wife of another public teacher, of almost equal eminence. All three concur in denouncing offenses against morality. "Hypocrisy is the tribute paid by vice to virtue." So be it. But I decline to

stand up as the "frightful example." I shall make
it my business to analyze some of these lives, and
will take my chances in the matter of libel suits.
I have no faith in critics. But I believe in public
justice.

VICTORIA WOODHULL.

New York, May 20, 1871.

According to Tilton, on the day this card was
published, he received word from Mrs. Woodhull
to call at her office, which he did, to have her inform him she meant Beecher and himself in the
allusion to public teachers of eminence, and proceeded to tell with vehement speech, a "wicked and
injurious story" which he sought by "many personal services and kindly attentions" to dissuade
her from publishing. These he continued until
April, 1872. He then stopped, but never explained
why the story, which he designed to suppress, was
finally printed in *Woodhull and Claflin's Weekly,*
November 2, 1872.

On the day the Beecher exposé was printed,
the paper also gave space to rumors reflecting on
Luther A. Challis, a broker. For this the two
women were arrested on a charge of sending improper matter through the mails, and locked up in
Ludlow Street jail in default of ten thousand dollars bail each. On the fourth, both were indicted.
Captain Blood was placed under arrest. Curiously,
an item in the evidence was the delivery, by a letter-
carrier, of several copies of the paper to the office of

the *Independent.* The prisoners were kept in durance for six weeks, but the case fell to the ground. George Francis Train, then at the beginning of his eccentricity, got himself locked up in the Tombs by printing and circulating excerpts from the Bible, that went much beyond Woodhull and Claflin in erotic expression. Stephen Pearl Andrews, a very liberal and able theosophical thinker, who held forth in Plymton Hall as the "Pantarch," was also jailed. The newspapers called it "a raid on the free-lovers."

Mrs. Woodhull's account of the six months' effort to protect Mr. Beecher, given to the *Chicago Times* during the church investigation, was rather fervid. "I ought to know Mr. Tilton," she was quoted as saying, "for he was my devoted lover for more than half a year, and I admit that during that time he was my accepted lover. A woman who could not love Theodore Tilton, especially in reciprocation of a generous, overwhelming affection such as he was capable of bestowing, must be indeed dead to all the sweeter impulses of our nature. I could not resist his inspiring fascinations."

The ingenious interviewer ventured to ask: "Do I understand, my dear madame, that the fascination was mutual and irresistible?"

"You will think so," she replied, "when I tell you that so enamored and infatuated with each other were we that for three months we were hardly out of each other's sight day or night. . . . **Of course we were lovers—devoted, true and faithful lovers.** Theodore was then estranged from his wife and undergoing all the agonies of the torture inflicted upon him by the treachery of his friend, Mr. Beecher."

In the course of her suffrage activities a very neat bit of presswork, acclaiming her story and purposes, had been put out. The interviewer ventured a further intimate inquiry, as to whether during this period of intensity Tilton "unlocked the secrets and griefs that beset his breast."

"Yes, sir," she answered, "we were very naturally mutually confiding. And it was during this time he wrote of me so eloquently in the little *brochure* of a biography from his pen."

Comparing the lively lady of his hectic affections with the others engaged in the suffrage cause, Tilton had written:

"Victoria C. Woodhull is a younger heroine than most of the foregoing, having come into the cause after some of her elders had already become veterans. But her advocacy of woman's rights to the ballot, as logically deduced from the Fourteenth and Fifteenth Amendments, has given her a national notoriety. If the women's movement has a Joan of Arc, it is this gentle, but fiery genius. She is one of the most remarkable women of her time. Little understood by the public, she is denounced in the most outrageous manner by people who do not appreciate her moral worth. But her

[219]

sincerity, her truthfulness, her uprightness, her true nobility of character, are so well known to those who know her well, that she ranks, in the estimation of these, somewhat as St. Theresa does in the admiring thoughts of pious Catholics. She is a devotee—a religious enthusiast—a seer of visions—a devout communionist with the other world. She acts under spiritual influence, and like St. Paul, is 'not disobedient to the heavenly vision.' Her bold social theories have startled many good souls, but anybody who, on this account, imagines her to stand below the whitest and purest of her sex, will misplace a woman who in her moral integrity rises to the full heights of the highest."

It might be explained that the *Weekly* did not come out weekly, and this issue of November second, was the first in some time. Besides their stay in Ludlow Street, the sisters were treated to a few days in the Tombs. Anthony Comstock, the celebrated vice hunter, was the prosecutor behind Challis, who had a case of his own. Comstock was after the paper because of its doctrines. No New York journal save the *Evening Telegram* gave space to the scandal at the moment. Mr. Beecher was credited with dismissing it by saying: "In passing along the way any one is liable to have a bucket of slops thrown upon him. It is disagreeable, but does no particular harm."

The case reached the Attorney-General of the United States, George H. Williams, who decided that they had violated no law. One was subsequently provided through the efforts of the zealous Comstock, but Woodhull and Claflin went free. Mrs. Woodhull was arrested once more as she lectured on "The Naked Truth," at Cooper Union, but underwent nothing worse than a few extra days in Ludlow Street jail, though "The Naked Truth" was something more than *décolleté*.

Meanwhile, the busybodies in the church could not let matters rest and die out. Tilton had ceased to attend services. "It was proposed," records Mr. Beecher, "to drop him from the list of members for non-attendance; and as he asserted to me his withdrawal, this might have been done, but his wife still attended the church and hoped for his restoration. I recollect having with him a conversation in which he dimly hinted to me that he thought it not unlikely he might go back to his old position. He seemed to be in a mood to regret the past."

This is super-ingenuous. William F. West, a member of Plymouth, was responsible for the proposition. Tilton later revealed that West came to him with a request that he join in an inquiry to get at the bottom of the scandal under the guise of investigating the reasons for his absenteeism. Tilton declined the bait. The persistent West, however, filed his charges, and they were presented to Tilton by a committee on October 6, 1873. His answer was that he had not attended the church for nearly four years, nor did either

himself or the pastor consider him a member thereof. A written copy of West's charges was then
sent to Tilton on October seventeenth, with a request for a reply by the twenty-third. He
answered on the twenty-seventh, that he had
terminated his connection with the church and
could not receive communications therefrom. The
committee reported all this at a meeting of the
Society, held on October thirty-first, with a rec-
ommendation that Tilton be dropped from the roll.
While this was under discussion, Brother West
having asked that Tilton be cited to appear before
a final vote was taken, that gentleman rose in person and remarked with amazing effrontery:

"If I have a right to speak here to-night I desire to say a few plain words. Twenty years ago I
joined this church, and many of the most precious
moments of my life center around these walls.
Four years ago I ceased my membership, nor have
I ever been from that time till to-night under this
roof. In retiring from Plymouth Church I did not
ask for the erasing of my name from the rolls because the circumstances were such that I could not
publicly state them without wounding the feelings
of others besides myself. During these years of my
absence, a story has filled the land, covering it like
a mist, that I had slandered the minister of this
church. Last summer Mr. Beecher published an
explicit card in the *Brooklyn Eagle* exempting me
from this injustice. Notwithstanding this public
disclaimer by him on my behalf, a committee of this

church by its action has given rise to injurious statements in the public press, that my claim of nonmembership is made by me in order to avoid my just responsibility to the church as a member. I have therefore come here to-night not from any obligation of membership, for I am not a member of the church, and not governed by any of its rules, and not because the committee has summoned me, but of my own free will, prompted by my self-respect, and as a matter vital to my life and honor, to say to Mr. Beecher, in this presence, surrounded here by his friends, that if I have slandered him I am ready to answer for it to the man whom I have slandered. If, therefore, the minister of this church has anything whereof to accuse me, let him now speak, and I shall answer as God is my judge."

Tart discussion followed in objection to this easy way of avoiding responsibility, which was stilled when Mr. Beecher took sides with Tilton, sustaining his right to assume that his voluntary and continued absence had freed him from obligations. He concluded: "I do not see that Mr. Tilton has ever tried to shrink from his proper responsibility. He asks if I have a charge to make against him. I have none. Whatever differences have existed between us have been amicably adjusted. So far as I am concerned they are buried, and so far as he is concerned, I am sure they are buried. This matter has been against my judgment from the beginning. I said to the people: 'You will only take this business up and

carry it on to a point where you can do nothing
and then leave it where you began.' I hold that
to-night. It is not wise and not according to my
judgment, and that which I held in the beginning,
I hold still."

There was much applause, but a persistent minority clung to a desire to smoke the scandal out
by a church trial of Tilton. They were over-
whelmed by a vote of two hundred and seventy-one
to twelve. Then the Reverend S. B. Halliday,
assistant pastor, moved that the church vote Mr.
Tilton a letter recommending him as a "strong,
Christian man." This did not get a second. The
meeting adjourned, "satisfied that Plymouth
Church had shaken herself free from the incubus
that had been fastened upon her for the last ten
months."

The event, unfortunately, proved that this was
not so. Under the leadership of Doctor R. S.
Storrs and Doctor William I. Budington, the
Church of the Pilgrims and the Clinton Avenue
Congregational Church, served a notice of their
intent to withdraw from association with a church
that had signally failed in its duty of disciplining
a recalcitrant member, to wit, the defiant Tilton.
The joint letter was presented at a meeting of
Plymouth Parish, held November 26, 1873. Its
purpose, obvious enough, as a further effort to
injure Mr. Beecher, failed. Plymouth decided to
stand alone by a vote of five hundred and four to
twenty-five.

BEECHER AND TILTON

The action of Doctor Storrs in this instance was keenly felt by Mr. Beecher, who, not long before, had received from him an expression of support and sympathy. Doctor Budington had all along been hostile. Mr. Beecher thought if Doctor Storrs had been favored with a bringing-up in Indiana, instead of Boston, he would have proved more open-minded. Their evident intent, of course, was to bring the scandal into the open, neither having faith in Mr. Beecher's innocence. The lack of orthodoxy in his teachings was also a considerable factor. The result was the exclusion of Plymouth from the Congregational council. Some remarks of the Reverend Leonard Bacon, who had been moderator of the body, made at New Haven, caused Tilton to take up the issue, putting his correspondence with Bacon, but not his charges against Beecher, into a statement which became public on June 24, 1874. In this, to vindicate himself, he quoted from Mr. Beecher's unlucky confidential note to Frank D. Moulton. Naturally, this forced the fight, especially as Tilton now professed a willingness to go to the bottom, even though it involved revealing the various confessions and counter-confessions of his weak-willed wife, who was sorely sinned against on all sides. The "Treaty" with Bowen had also become public, at the instance, Tilton alleged, of Mr. Beecher. He thought he was being overloaded with odium.

The situation now became unendurable for

Mr. Beecher. He accordingly, on July 7, 1874, advised the Examining Board of Plymouth Church that he had, on June twenty-seventh, requested Henry W. Sage, Augustus Storrs, Henry M. Cleveland, from the church, and Horace B. Claflin, John Winslow and Stephen Van Cullen White, from the Society, to examine into the "rumors, insinuations or charges," respecting his conduct. He asked the committee to confirm his selections, which it did. The gentlemen were all eminent. Mr. White became famous later as a deacon who plunged violently in Wall Street, lost his fortune and studied stars from a private observatory on Columbia Heights. The committee at once took up the work of inquiry, summoning Tilton, Moulton, et al., before it. Tilton filed a sworn affidavit covering the long course of the scandal. Summed up, he charged that:

Henry Ward Beecher, as pastor and friend of Mr. Tilton and family, trespassed upon the sanctity of friendship and hospitality in a long endeavor to seduce Mrs. Elizabeth R. Tilton, that by the artful use of his priestly authority with her, she being his pupil in religion, he accomplished this seduction; that for a period of a year and a half, or thereabout, he maintained criminal intercourse with her, overcoming her previous modest scruples against such conduct by investing it with a false justification as sanctioned by love and religion; that he then participated in a conspiracy to degrade Theodore Tilton before the public by loss of place, business

BEECHER AND TILTON

and repute; that he abused Mr. Tilton's forgiveness and pledge of protection by thereafter authorizing a series of measures by Plymouth Church having for their object the putting of a stigma upon Mr. Tilton before the church, and also before an ecclesiastical council, insomuch that the moderator of that council, interpreting these acts by Mr. Beecher and his church, declared publicly that they showed Mr. Beecher to be the most magnanimous of men and Mr. Tilton to be a knave and a dog.

The affidavit was prefaced with a statement, signed by Tilton, which St. Clair McKelway once told me he wrote. McKelway was then an editorial writer on the *Eagle* and in Tilton's confidence. It certainly bears all the earmarks of his style. It was made public in the *Brooklyn Argus* of Tuesday, August 21, 1874, for the evident purpose of influencing the report of the Plymouth committee, but failed to influence that body, reporting on August twenty-fourth:

We find from the evidence that Mr. Beecher has never committed any unchaste or improper act with Mrs. Tilton, nor made any unchaste or improper remark, proffer, or solicitation to her of any kind or description whatever.

If this were a question of errors of judgment on the part of Mr. Beecher, it would be easy to criticize, especially in the light of recent events. In such criticism, even to the extent of regrets and censure, we are sure no man would join more sincerely than Mr. Beecher himself.

[227]

THE DREADFUL DECADE

We find nothing whatever in the evidence that should impair the perfect confidence of Plymouth Church or the world in the Christian character and integrity of Henry Ward Beecher.

And now let the peace of God, that passeth all understanding, rest and abide with Plymouth Church and her beloved and eminent pastor, so much and so long afflicted.

The prayer for peace was not productive. Tilton now began an action in one hundred thousand dollars damages against Mr. Beecher for alienating his wife's affections. The church rose solidly behind its pastor and resolved to see him through. As a counter-move, Tilton and Frank D. Moulton were indicted for criminal libel by the Kings County Grand Jury on October third. Tilton's case against Beecher came to trial before Judge Joseph Neilson, in the City Court of Brooklyn, January 6, 1875, and proved to be the longest drawn-out cause in the history of American jurisprudence.

Tilton's counsel were eminent, led by ex-Judge William Fullerton and William A. Beach, who had for support General Roger A. Pryor, Samuel D. Morris and Thomas E. Pearsall, the last two being Brooklyn lawyers. Mr. Beecher was defended by William M. Evarts, Thomas G. Shearman, General Benjamin F. Tracy, John W. Sterling, John C. Porter and John L. Hill. The testimony taken covered three thousand pages.

BEECHER AND TILTON

The trial attracted world-wide attention. It was reported literally by the newspapers, the *Brooklyn Eagle* even making an innovation in its method of printing by inserting last minute testimony in a mortise cut in its back page stereotype. It ended in a disagreement, June 24, 1875, after the jury had wrangled for nine days, standing nine to three in favor of the defendant. It was never retried, and the criminal libel cases were dropped. Both sides had more than enough.

Whether innocent or guilty of the charge, Mr. Beecher outrode the storm. His wife, friends and church stood by him. The *Life of Christ,* however, was "knocked higher than a kite." The second volume was never published, and the failure of the undertaking sent the publishers, Fords, Howard and Hurlburt, into bankruptcy, while Samuel Wilkinson who had bought the rights and plates of the bankrupts for sixty thousand dollars lost his money. The *Christian Union* fell into the hands of Doctor Lyman Abbott and became the *Outlook.*

Mr. Beecher continued powerful in his pulpit. Plymouth could still be located by the Sunday throngs marching to its services. He had a conspicuous part in electing Seth Low as the reform mayor of Brooklyn, in 1881, and was a potent factor in the success of Grover Cleveland in 1884, when he became a leading "mugwump," as the independents of the day were dubbed. In 1886, with Mrs. Beecher, he visited England and was received with great acclaim by W. E. Gladstone and the British public. He died from a stroke of apoplexy, Tuesday, March 8, 1887, at the age of seventy-four, having been born June 24, 1813, at Litchfield, Connecticut, ninth of the remarkable children of Lyman Beecher and Roxana Foote Beecher.

Perhaps Mr. Beecher's successful survival was the triumph of virtue over wrong-doing; equally so, it may have been that of a strong personality outweighing a weaker one. Certainly ill fortune followed Theodore Tilton. The *Golden Age* faded out and *Tempest Tossed* in book form was not a great seller. He continued to have some vogue as a lecturer, but finally gave up the fight and exiled himself to France. He died in Paris, May 25, 1907, from the effects of an attack of pneumonia. He was buried in Barbizon. His small estate—three thousand dollars—was left to his two daughters, Mrs. William H. Pelton and Mrs. John E. Gardin. He was that rarity, a native New Yorker, having been born in that city, October 2, 1835.

Mrs. Tilton died at the house of her daughter, Mrs. Pelton, 1403 Pacific Street, Brooklyn, April 13, 1897. She was born Elizabeth M. Richards. Dismissed from Plymouth Church in 1878, she had affiliated with a group calling itself the Plymouth Brotherhood, which met at her house. Seven children were born to the Tiltons, of whom the daughters named above and two sons, Ralph and Carroll, only, grew to maturity; both sons died before the father. Ralph possessed much talent and at the time of his decease was editor of the *Delineator.* A woman killed herself to follow him to the grave. Moulton, the "mutual friend," losing caste and money, slipped beneath the surface. *Exeunt omnes!*

The luck of Mrs. Woodhull and Miss Claflin did not fail them. Following the Beecher-Tilton trial, being possessed of considerable money, it would appear, the two shrewd sisters went to England. Here, in 1878, Mrs. Woodhull married John Biddulph Martin, a wealthy London banker. He died at Las Palmas, Canary Islands, on March 20, 1897. They resided on a great estate in Worcestershire, where, after the husband's death, Mrs. Martin carried on many philanthropic activities, and in 1914, offered a five thousand dollar cash prize and a silver trophy for a trans-Atlantic air flight. She also gave five thousand dollars toward celebrating the one hundredth anniversary of peace between England and America. She further edited and published a magazine, the *Humanitarian.* The Martin London home was a fine house at 17 Hyde Park Gate. Her name was used by the American suffrage movers in 1892, as a candidate for president, who, of course, could receive no votes. Her husband left her a fortune rated at seven hundred fifty thousand dollars. Out of her wealth she generously contributed to the purchase of Sulgrave Manor, home of George Washington's ancestors, and now owned by the association of that name. She was last seen in New York on November 20, 1893, when she lectured at Carnegie Hall on "The Scientific Propagation of the Human Race." She was then elderly, spectacled, vigorous-looking and old-fashioned. The lecture was a sensible talk. She established her social status in England with a firm hand, compelling the British Museum to remove books from its shelves that contained reflections on her character, though receiving but twenty shillings in damages.

Miss Claflin, with equal success in the matrimonial market, married Sir Francis Cook, who possessed the Portuguese title of Marquis of Montserrat and a marvelous estate at Cintra, in Portugal. He accumulated great wealth as an importer of India shawls to England. They had been made fashionable by Queen Victoria. At his death in 1901, Sir Francis left his widow two million dollars, which she enjoyed until January 18, 1923, when her life ended in London.

CHAPTER VII

INDIAN WARS

Forsyth's Frontier Fight—Modocs Murder Peace Commissioners—
The Sioux Troubles—Complete Destruction of General George A.
Custer's Command—Sitting Bull's Success—Escape to Canada.

DURING the Civil War period the advance of
settlers into the territories of the farther West had
been checked. Indians and the buffalo, on which
the wild people of the plains subsisted, were left
to live together as before the white man came.
But with peace between the states, covered wagons
began moving again and settling was further
stimulated by land bounties to ex-soldiers and the
sale of lands that had been granted to railroads.
The completion of the Union Pacific cut the con-
tinent in two. These bands of iron meant death
to the buffalo, and war and enforced migrations or
dispersal to the tribes.

This the Indians sensed and became so aggres-
sive as to require the attention of the best talent in
the regular army, acting to enforce a policy of
putting the red men on reservations and making
them government wards. The bands nearest to
civilization and most degraded by contact with the
whites were easily sequestered, but the bold

Pawnees, Comanches and Cheyennes resisted and painted the plains with blood. General P. H. Sheridan was given command of the Department of the Missouri, with headquarters at Fort Harker, Kansas, to rein in the unruly reds. One of the most interesting of the resulting adventures was the fight between a body of fifty picked scouts, under Colonel George A. Forsyth and Lieutenant Frederick H. Beecher, and a band of nearly one thousand Cheyennes and some Brulé and Ogallala dog soldiers at a point on the Republican River in Northwestern Kansas that began on the evening of September 16, 1868, and lasted for ten days. The company had been scouting in a leisurely way amid plentiful Indian signs and had come to camp at evening on the bank of the stream, opposite a small island. At dusk they suddenly became aware of the near-by presence of an Indian host, and making for the island "dug in" for the night.

When day came, they saw themselves hopelessly outnumbered. Their horses were soon killed by Indian fire. Lieutenant Beecher, a Civil War hero, who had been lamed at Gettysburg, nephew of Henry Ward Beecher, was mortally wounded and soon died. Three scouts, G. W. Chalmers, William Wilson and Chalmers Smith, were dead. Assistant-Surgeon J. H. Mooers was fatally hurt and unable to aid the injured, among whom was Forsyth himself with a broken leg, a ball in his thigh and a skull cracked by a grazing shot. The

Indians, led by Roman Nose, a great warrior, attempted to rush the island on their ponies, but the fire of the defenders was too deadly. They drew off and prepared for a siege. Roman Nose fell in the charge and the death song was the only music heard by the besieged. Forsyth contrived to send four men to Fort Wallace, two of whom arrived in the nick of time to bring Colonel L. H. Carpenter with a rescuing force before which the warriors declined to stand. The Cheyennes had considered themselves invincible. The incident changed their minds.

On April 11, 1873, a tragic affair occurred in the long list of troubles with the American Indians. In Siskiyou County, California, bordering on Oregon, lived the small tribe called Modocs. They had made their home on good lands lining Tule Lake and first came into contact with the whites in 1848-9, when many gold-seekers came to California by way of the Oregon trail. There was no clash until 1853, when Indians of the Pitt River tribe slaughtered a number of emigrants near Alturas and one James Crosby organized a company of rangers to hunt them down. Some Modocs came into Crosby's camp and at night the Pitt River braves crept in and surprised the sleepers, wounding a small number with arrows. This was unfairly laid to Modoc treachery, and eleven out of a party of fourteen were wantonly slain. The usual reprisals followed, innocent emigrants fall-

ing victims to the feud. Troubles in the way of
stock stealing and the like continued until, in 1869,
the government decided to round up the Modocs
on the Klamath reservation in Oregon. The
Modocs did not like the Klamaths, but yielded to
pressure. Friction with the Klamaths soon followed. Captain O. C. Knapp, the Indian agent,
handled the situation tactlessly, with the result that
the Modocs, under Captain Jack, their chief, left
Klamath and returned to their old grounds on
Lost River. There was no more trouble for the
moment, and so matters rested until November 28,
1872, when William W. Belknap, Secretary of
War, ordered Major James Jackson, in command
at Fort Klamath, to round up the Modocs and
take them back to the reservation, using such force
as might be necessary. Jackson went on his mis-
sion the next day in command of a company of
cavalry.

The Indians met them fully armed, but at
Jackson's request, all laid aside their weapons,
save one, Scar-Faced Charley, who kept an old
revolver in his belt. Jackson ordered his First
Lieutenant, Boutelle, to take the pistol. He made
the demand roughly and profanely. Scar-Faced
Charley replied that he was not a dog and would
keep his gun. Boutelle drew his own revolver and
the two fired at the same moment, Scar-Faced
Charley's bullet boring a hole through Boutelle's
coat. The warriors reached for their rifles as the

soldiers began a rapid fusillade. One cavalryman was killed, and one warrior, called Watchman. Half a dozen were wounded on both sides. The soldiers fled, but some settlers rallied and continued the affray. A Modoc man, a fifteen-year-old girl, three little children and one warrior were killed. An aged Modoc woman was burned to death. Three settlers lost their lives in the onset. Bloody work followed. By night the Modocs began hunting men. They killed eighteen.

The open lands were now untenable and the desperate band took refuge in a disheveled region called the Lava Beds, a twisted, volcanic desolation rich in secure hiding-places. Here they were left unmolested for two weeks, when the government began to hunt them out. This was in mid-January, 1873. On the seventeenth, a skirmish occurred, the warriors winning, the soldiers and settlers losing a number of men. The campaign rested.

Finding the task too difficult, the government appointed a Peace Commission composed of Major-General E. R. S. Canby, a distinguished Civil War soldier, A. B. Meacham, Doctor Eleazer Thomas and L. S. Dyar, Judge A. M. Roseborough, his partner, Mr. Steele, and John Fairchilds, a rancher. All of these were friendly with the Modocs and they agreed to attempt the arranging of a conference. They met Captain Jack and his braves on February 28, 1873, who promised to meet the commissioners at Fairchilds' the next day, and did so. On March tenth, a truce was arranged, pending an adjustment by further conferences. The military force under Brigadier-General A. C. Gillem, now numbering some five hundred men, grouped nearer. Some Indian ponies were taken. When their owners demanded them, they were told that they would be returned when final peace came. The councils continued inconclusively. No progress was made, the Indians becoming more surly and suspicious. On the tenth, an unsatisfactory session was held, after which Winema, the Modoc wife of Frank Riddle, the commissioners' interpreter, visited the tribe and heard rumors that if the commissioners came again, they would be killed. Canby was warned accordingly, but insisted on a meeting on the eleventh. That morning Messrs. Canby, Meacham, Thomas and Dyar, with Riddle and Winema, met Captain Jack, Boston Charley, John Schonchin, Boncho, Bogus Charley, Black Jim, Hooker Jim and Slolux, the chief men of the tribe. Canby opened with a very conciliatory talk, and wished the Indians to understand that the "white man's law" was "straight and strong." Captain Jack drew a wriggle in the dust with a stick and replied: "General Canby, your law is crooked as this." He then charged that the truce had been broken by the bringing of more soldiers and posting them to better advantage. He demanded that the soldiers be taken away or he would not talk peace, asking further that his people be allowed homes on Hot Creek.

"Do you agree to what I ask of you or not?" he queried sternly of Canby. "Tell me. I am tired of waiting for you to speak." Meacham begged Canby to promise Jack, for "heaven's sake," seeing the menace in the Indian's eyes. He did not respond, but Schonchin repeated the demand to Meacham, who said he would ask the Great Father at Washington to do it.

Before this could be turned into Modoc by Riddle, Captain Jack said curtly in his own tongue: "Ut wih kutt"—meaning, "All ready, do it." He fired at Canby with a pistol, the bullet striking under his right eye. The general ran. Bogus Charley tripped him, and when he fell, cut his throat. Boston Charley shot Doctor Thomas. Meacham received seven shot wounds, none serious. He fell, however. The Indians now stripped all three of their victims, Captain Jack taking the general's uniform and sword. Boston Charley started to scalp the wounded Meacham, but Winema threw herself on his body and saved his life, like a second Pocahontas. A cry that the soldiers were coming caused the murderers to flee. Meacham soon recovered.

The troops now began an active effort to capture the assassins and the tribe. General Jeff C. Davis took command. The Modocs held out until May twenty-eighth, when fifteen surrendered.

THE DREADFUL DECADE

On June second, Captain Jack and fifteen others gave up. In the two parties were all the Indians concerned in the murder. This surrender was not brought about without some fighting, in which eight soldiers were killed and twenty wounded.

General Davis had determined to hang about a dozen of the men, but the government ordered their trial by a military commission. The result of this order was much dissatisfaction among the Oregon settlers who waylaid a train conveying seventeen Modocs to Fort Klamath and killed a number of them. The commission went into session at Fort Klamath on July 5, 1873. When Captain Jack was called upon to state his defense he said:

I see that I have no show, my days are gone. When I was a boy, I had it in my heart to be a friend to the white people. I was a friend to them until three months ago. Some of these very men are here to-day, at liberty, free men, while I am here in irons. Life is mine only for a short time. I know it, I feel it. The reason I say these words is this. Some of my men voted to kill the commissioners. I fought it with all of my might. I begged them not to kill unarmed men. What did they finally do? They threw me down, placed a woman's hat on my head, pointed at me, saying, "Squaw, squaw! Lie there. You may not take any part in our plot. That's all right, be not afraid that you will die with a soldier's bullet. We will save that trouble for the soldier now." What could

I do? My life was at stake, no matter which way I might turn, so I agreed to do the coward's act, which the world knows this day. All I wish is that my side of the story may be told. I am not afraid to die, but I must say, I am ashamed to die the way that I am to die, with my hands tied behind me. Ashamed is not the right expression. I once thought that I would die on the battle-field, defending my rights and home that was mine, given to me by no man. Judge Roseborough and Squire Steele of Yreka were both men. They gave me good advice. I shall carry their words in my heart, to the last moment of my life. I feel not that I am defeated rightly. The very men that drove me to kill Canby, gave themselves up and then ran me down. If I had only known what they were doing, you men would not have had me here to-day with chains on my legs and with satisfied smiles on your faces, for I would have died fighting, but my people lied to me, so I would not shoot them. The men that I speak of are here now free. They fought for their liberty with my life. They all did just as bad deeds as I did when I killed that noble man Canby. I see it is too late to repent now. It is my duty to give some explanation, so the White Father may know something of what caused me to fall. So I will say again, hoping that at least a few of my words may become known to the white people. I see no crime in my heart, although I killed Canby. But why did I do it? Do you understand? I was forced to do it. I did it to save my life for a while. I thought I would die on the battle-field fighting you white soldiers. You white people have driven me from mountain to mountain, from valley to valley, as

[241]

we do the wounded deer. At last you have got me here. I see but a few days more ahead of me. If I had got a lawyer when my trial commenced, I do not think that I and these other men would be the only ones that would have been condemned to die. The very men that are free to-day would have surely been with us right now.

What talk I put up is no good. Why, I am a murderer! Everybody says that. That is so. Do I deny the charge? No, I do not. I did it, but I say again I had to do it. Now for the last time, I say again, I am ashamed of my coming death, but not afraid. What our White Father says is right. I must die, so this is all. I have no more to say. I see in your faces you are tired of listening to me. Perhaps some of you think I am lying, but, my friends, I tell the truth. I shall feel for the welfare of my young boys and girls. I hope the white people will not ill treat them on my account, for they can not help what wrongs I did. That is the one matter, and the only matter that bothers me, is my young people. I hope the White Father at Washington will give them a good house and start them in life. If the government will give them a chance, they will show or prove that the government's efforts will not be in vain.

The government ought to care for my young people. See the good land and the size of my country that is taken away from me and my people. If I wanted to talk more, I could do so and tell you facts and prove them by white people, that would open the eyes of all of you that are here to-day, about the way my people have been murdered by the whites. I will say, not one white man was ever punished for his deeds. If the white people that killed our women and children had been tried and punished, I would not have thought so much of myself and companions. Could I? Could I? Please answer. No, you men answer me not. Do we Indians stand any show for justice with you white people, with your own laws? I say no. I know it. You people can shoot any of us Indians any time you want to whether we are in war or in peace. Can any of you tell me where ever any man has been punished in the past for killing a Modoc in cold blood? No, you can not tell me. I am on the edge of my grave; my life is in your people's hands. I charge the white people of wholesale murder. Not only once, but many times. Think about Ben Wright. What did he do? He killed nearly fifty of my people. Among the killed was my father. He was holding a peace council with them. Was he or any of his men punished? No, not one. Mind you, Ben Wright and his men were civilized white people. The other civilized white people at Yreka, California, made a big hero of him, gave him a fine dinner and a big dance in his honor for murdering innocent Indians. He was praised for his crime. Now here I am. Killed one man, after I had been fooled by him many times and forced to do the act by my own warriors. The law says, "Hang him. He is nothing but an Indian, anyhow. We can kill them any time for nothing, but this one has done something, so hang him." Why did not the white man's law say that about Ben Wright? So now I do quit talking. In a few days I shall be no more. I now bid the world farewell.

The commission sentenced Captain Jack, Bos-

ton Charley, Black Jim, Schonchin, Boncho and
Slolux to death. The two last were reprieved at the
foot of the scaffold. The others were hanged under army auspices at Fort Klamath on October 3,
1873. Schonchin's brother came to him at the gallows and said:

I came here not to bid you farewell, but to see
if you die like a man. I see you lack courage. I
see tears in your eyes. You would not, and did
not, listen to me, so now I say I cast you to the
four winds. You are no brother of mine. You put
a black mark upon my name, although my word
was as true as the sun. So now die. I cast you
away.

The handful of survivors were taken to the Indian territory. By act of Congress, approved
March 3, 1909, the few Modocs surviving as the
descendants of the tribe were allowed to return to
Klamath where allotments were provided. Nearly
all went back, but a few families returned to
Oklahoma.

While the plains Indians were decidedly inferior to those east of the Alleghanies, the great
Siouan family was the most powerful survival of
the tribes, and still, in a large measure, independent, in the mid-seventies. It was estimated that
the various clans of the Sioux could raise twelve
thousand fighting men. They were well-armed
and in a region still abounding in buffalo and

other game. The land of the Dakotas was distant from civilization and savage ways still ruled.

The discovery of gold in the Black Hills and the beginning of the Northern-Pacific Railway led to an Indian outbreak of large proportions in 1874, when the Sioux, who had been concentrated in the Dakotas, after the Minnesota outbreak of 1863, rose in part to resist the invasion of the white men. The two most important chiefs, Red Cloud and Spotted Tail, were placated and kept order in the sphere of their influence, but some two thousand lodges chose to follow the political leadership of Sitting Bull, a medicine-man of influence, who had with him many of the younger warriors and numerous fighting chiefs, notably Rain-in-the-Face, Crazy Horse and Young-Man-Afraid-of-Horses. They were well-armed, well-mounted and accomplished in the arts of savage warfare. The best talent in the regular army was sent against them—master soldiers like George Crook, Alfred H. Terry, John Gibbon, J. S. Brisbin, Marcus A. Reno, Nelson A. Miles and George A. Custer. All had been general officers in the Civil War. These the Indians successfully evaded for months, leading the regulars many weary miles, picking off stragglers and doing about as they pleased, to the great discomfort of the military gentlemen. The Cheyennes, Comanches and Arapahoes also made trouble.

In the spring of 1876, Terry was set to the task

of rounding up the recalcitrants, who were known to be in the Yellowstone country in the vicinity of the river's juncture with the Little Big Horn, in the then territory of Montana. By the first of May the troops reached the Yellowstone region and began the complicated task of finding Sitting Bull and his followers.

The regulars groped vainly amid the hills for some sight of the Sioux, marching miles in vain pursuit, until, exasperated by ill success, Custer took eight companies of the Seventh Cavalry and plunged independently into the wilderness, abandoning communications and leaving his superiors in the dark both as to his purposes and accomplishments.

Meanwhile the major body, under Generals Terry and Gibbon, were creeping along the rivers, tugging a battery of Gatlings in an effort to locate the elusive foe. They were seldom out of sight of the enemy, but never observed one of them. Soldiers who strayed were killed and scalped, but no assault in force was indulged in. The road daily grew more difficult and the problem more perplexing. There was no word of Custer and no sign of the Sioux. A vivid picture of the trying advance is found in the journal kept by Lieutenant James H. Bradley, published in the proceedings of the Montana Historical Society for 1896. Writing under date of June 25, 1876, he observes:

At four A. M., in compliance with orders, I sent
six Crows up Tullock's Fork, and half an hour
later followed with the remainder of the Crows and
my detachment. At five-thirty A. M. the command
broke camp and marched two miles up Tullock's
Fork and then turned off to the right into the hills,
expecting to find a comparatively level table-land
leading to the Little Big Horn. Meantime, I had
ascended the stream nine miles, when I halted to
await some indication that I was being followed by
the command, and after a long delay, was overtaken by a squad of cavalry sent to notify me of the
change of route. I soon rejoined, taking a short
cut across the hills, and found the command involved in a labyrinth of bald hills and deep, precipitous ravines completely destitute of water.
The men had emptied their canteens of the
wretched alkali water they started with and were
parched with thirst as well as greatly fatigued
with clambering over such ground. A worse route
could not have been chosen, but destitute of a guide
as we were, it is not to be wondered that we en-
tangled ourselves in such a mesh of physical obstacles.

While the command struggled on toward the
Big Horn as the nearest point of escape, I
executed an order given me by General Terry to
scout to a distant ridge on the left of our line of
march, from which it was thought the Little Big
Horn might be seen, and possibly, an Indian camp.
Reaching the ridge after an exceedingly toilsome
march of eight miles over a very rough country, I
found myself confronted by another ridge a few
miles farther on that completely obstructed the
view. Having been ordered not to pass the first

[247]

ridge, I turned back and overtook the infantry battalion at six-fifty P. M., just as they were going into camp in the valley of the Big Horn. There I learned that some of the Crows who had gone up Tullock's Fork in the morning had discovered a smoke in the direction of the Little Big Horn, which was thought to indicate the presence of the Sioux village, and the cavalry and Gatling battery, accompanied by General Terry, were pushing on with a view of getting as near it as possible to-night. The infantry, which had already marched twenty-three miles, were tc remain in camp for the night, and follow in the morning.

I joined the cavalry with my detachment, orders having been left for me to that effect. A brisk rain set in toward evening, and continued to fall in successive showers through the first half of the night. Darkness overtook us still pushing on up the Big Horn, and though the march had been difficult by day, it was doubly so in the darkness of the night. The cavalry officers who scouted up the Big Horn last April were acting as guides, for want of better, and as their knowledge of the country was far from profound, we were continually encountering serious obstacles to our march—now a precipitous hillside, now a deep ravine. Occasionally as the head of the column was checked, we would find ourselves closed up in a dense mass, and again where the path grew narrow, we would stretch out in an attenuated thread, the men in the rear racing desperately after those in front not to lose sight of them in the gloom, and be left without a clue to the direction they had taken. Every now and then a long halt was made, as an avenue of escape was sought from some topographical net in which we had become involved.

There was great danger at times, when the column stretched out to unusual length, that it would become broken and leave us scattered over the country in a dozen bewildered fragments, and once the cry did go up, "The battery is missing." A halt was made, and after some racing and hallooing, the missing guns were set right again, having lost the human thread, and so wandered a mile or so out of the way. At another time, some of the cavalry went astray, and lost half an hour getting back to us.

At length, after hours of such toil, getting out of one difficulty only to plunge at once into another, the head of the column came plump on the brink of a precipice at whose feet swept the roaring waters of the Big Horn. The water gleamed in front, a hundred and fifty feet below, and to the right hand and to the left the ground broke off into a steep declivity down which nothing could be seen but forbidding gloom. Our cavalry guides were wholly bewildered, and everybody was tired out, and dripping with wet, and impatient to get somewhere and rest. When General Terry saw the walls of Fort Fisher before him, he knew what to do. He threw his battalions against them, carried them by storm, and gained a glorious victory and won a star; but when he saw to what a pass we had now come, and reflected that every step we took seemed only to render our situation more perplexing, he appeared uncertain and irresolute. For several minutes we sat our horses looking by turn at the water and into the black ravines, when I ventured to suggest to the general that we trust ourselves to the guidance of Little Face, one of my Crow scouts who had roamed this country as a boy fifty years ago and had previously assured me that he knew every foot of it. Little Face was called up, said he could guide us to a good camping-ground, was accepted as a guide, and led off in the dark with as much confidence as though he was in the full light of day. The aimless, profitless scrambling was over; he conducted us by an easy route a mile or two to the left, where we found ourselves in a commodious valley with water enough in its little channel to suffice for drinking purposes. There was not much grass for the animals, but it was the best we could do without going several miles farther, and so, about midnight, we halted, unsaddled, and threw our weary forms down on the ground for a little rest, the cavalry having marched about thirty-five miles, and my detachment, in consequence of its diversions from the main column, about fifty-five.

The situation was somber enough, but the next day they were to learn the terrible truth. To quote Bradley further:

Monday twenty-sixth. Major Brisbin, who in General Gibbon's absence commands the column, roused me up this morning at daylight and ordered me out on a scout at once, not allowing my men to get breakfast. As I had traveled some twenty miles farther yesterday than anybody else, so that my horses were tired and my men hungry, it struck me as rather rough treatment. I was too much vexed to hurry much, and did not get off till four A. M., having sent six Crows ahead half an hour earlier. My orders were to scout to the Little Big Horn, looking out for Sioux signs and sending back word of any important discoveries. Having advanced about three miles, we entered a valley cut by a dry creek, and here came upon the fresh tracks of four ponies. As we entered the ravine, we saw a heavy smoke rising in our front, apparently fifteen or twenty miles away, and I at once concluded we were approaching the Sioux village, and that the trail had been made by a party of scouts therefrom.

Sending back a written report of the discovery, I took the trail of the four supposed Sioux in the hope of catching them in the Big Horn valley, toward which the trail led, and where we thought they might have camped, as there was no convenient way of leaving the valley into which they had gone except that by which they had entered it.

At the distance of less than two miles the trail struck the river, and we found that they had there crossed, leaving behind a horse and several articles of personal equipment, indicating that they had fled in great haste. An examination of the articles disclosed to our great surprise that they belonged to some of the Crows whom I had furnished to General Custer at the mouth of the Rosebud, which rendered it probable that the supposed Sioux were some of our own scouts who had for some reason left Custer's command and were returning to the Crow agency. While speculating upon the circumstances, three men were discovered on the opposite side of the Big Horn, about two miles away, apparently watching our movements. We at once signaled to them, with blankets, that we were friends, for a long time to no purpose, but when we were about to give up and seek some other method of communicating with them, they responded by kindling a fire that sent up a small column of smoke, indicating that they had seen signals and trusted our assurances. We gathered wet sage-brush and assured them with a similar smoke, and soon afterward they came down to the river and talked across the stream with Little Face and one or two more of the scouts who went down to meet them. While the interview went on, I kept the remainder of the detachment on the bluffs. Presently our Indians turned back and, as they came, shouted out at the top of their voices a doleful series of cries and wails that the interpreter, Bravo, explained was a song of mourning for the dead. That it boded some misfortune, there was no doubt; and when they came up, shedding copious tears and appearing pictures of misery, it was evident that the occasion was of no common sort. Little Face, in particular, wept with a bitterness of anguish such as I have rarely seen. For a while he could not speak, but at last composed himself and told his story in a choking voice, broken with frequent sobs. As he proceeded, the Crows one by one broke off from the group of listeners and going aside a little distance, sat down alone, weeping and chanting that dreadful mourning song, and rocking their bodies to and fro. They were the first listeners to the horrid story of the Custer massacre, and, outside of the relatives and personal friends of the fallen, there was none in this whole horrified nation of forty millions of people to whom the tidings brought greater grief.

In this fashion came the first intelligence of the great disaster. After the shock of the ill tidings, the young officers grew incredulous and optimistic. Such a thing could not be possible. It was all nonsense; the Crows were cowards who had skedaddled before knowing the result. Terry alone sat on his horse, silent and thoughtful. They were in great peril, and his soldier's sense told him so.

Terry and Gibbon pushed on at all speed over the hard country, marching on June twenty-sixth twenty-nine miles in a single day. The next morning brought them to a spot bordering the left bank of the Little Big Horn. Here they found the site of what had been a large Indian village bordering the stream for three miles. Several funeral lodges were standing, with slaughtered horses around them, containing the bodies of nine chiefs, while fragments of cavalry equipment lay all about. Soon they came upon bodies. The first to be found were those of Lieutenant Donald McIntosh, interpreter of the command, and Charlie Reynolds, one of the guides. A glove belonging to Captain George W. Yates was also discovered. High up on a slope they reached a scene of conflict, dotted with the bodies of men and horses. This was General Reno's battle-ground. One of Reno's scouts arrived with a fearful tale. They had come just in time to save Reno from destruction. He was found intrenched and anxiously awaiting the next move of the warriors. His wounded were cared for, and a strong column sent scouting down the river, where they found awaiting them a sight to appall the stoutest heart. About three miles below, on the right bank of the stream where the bluffs come sharply down to the water, they are interspersed with numerous ravines, among which the futile fighting had taken place. Here, huddled in a narrow compass, dead men and horses were piled promiscuously. At the highest point on the ridge lay Custer, surrounded by a devoted band: His two brothers, Captain Thomas W. Custer and Benjamin, a civilian; his nephew, Autie Reed, and his brother-in-law, Captain James Calhoun, and Captains Yates, Cooke and Smith, all in a narrow circle, their horses dead beside them. With Yates' company the last stand had been made. Every officer and man of the five companies were slain. They had successively thrown themselves across the path of the enemy, each to be annihilated in turn.

Custer had reached the river on the twenty-fifth of June, having marched all day and night. Reno had been detached with three companies, while Custer went on to his death. The Indians fell upon Reno, who was joined by Colonel Benteen with three more companies, in the nick of time. They saved themselves for the moment by intrenching, but had fifty-six killed and fifty-one wounded. Those rescued by Terry numbered three hundred twenty-nine. Had he not come when he did, they would have shared the fate of Custer's force. The latter's companies were C, E,

INDIAN WARS

F, I and L. Those with Reno were A, G and M.
Benteen's were D, H and K. Custer's five companies included thirteen officers and one hundred
ninety-one enlisted men. All lost their lives as did
four civilians.

Upon the body of a trooper lying at the border
of the field, was found Custer's last message,
stained with blood from the body of the slain
soldier and pierced with bullets. So much of it
as was legible read:

RENO

for god's sake send help
I am surrounded and can't
break through I have only
40 troopers left and cant hold
out another minute I   nt
send   lan to you as he's
dead   enough bucks

evacuate you   osition
join me for gods sake
hurry. Am entrenched along
the Big horn Basin

Custer.

Besides Custer and his brothers, the officers
killed included Captains Miles W. Keogh, who had
joined as a volunteer, and George W. Yates;
Lieutenants Sturgis, W. W. Cooke, Donald
McIntosh, B. H. Hodgson, H. M. Harrington,

Algernon E. Smith, James E. Porter, James Calhoun and W. Reilly. One newspaper correspondent, Kellogg of the *New York Herald,* also lost his life.

Who were the men who laid down their lives in the disaster? A letter addressed to the Honorable John W. Weeks, Secretary of War, in mid-March, 1925, brought this reply from Robert C. Davis, Adjutant-General:

The War Department has never published or compiled a list of the officers and men (about two hundred fifty in number) who were killed in the Custer Massacre; and, because of the pressure of current business and the limited clerical force available for its transaction, the preparation of such a list is impracticable.

Many gruesome legends have sprung up around the fight, from which but two living things escaped—Curley, a young Crow scout, who made use of a Sioux blanket to disguise himself and slipped away unharmed early in the mêlée; and Comanche, Captain Miles Keogh's dapple-gray horse, who was found by the rescuing soldiers with a gash on his flank, but otherwise quite well. He was kept at ease at Fort Niobrara the rest of his days. So no one from the Custer side of the conflict could tell anything. All Curley knew was that there was a lot of fighting, and that he escaped. Other Crows had left the command earlier, being

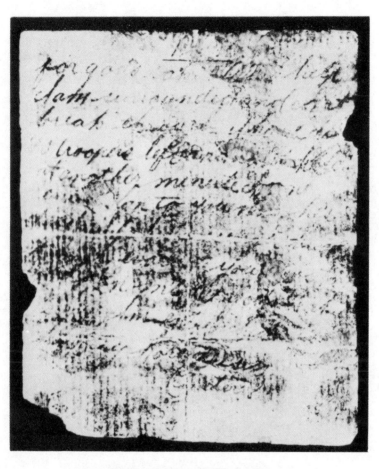

CUSTER'S LAST MESSAGE
Facsimile of the Original in the Collection
of OWEN D. YOUNG, ESQ.

certain that it was going to its doom. One of the legends was to the effect that Rain-in-the-Face killed Captain Tom Custer, the general's brother, and ate his heart in fulfillment of a vow of vengeance. Now a boyhood friend of mine, Judge Harry Ernest, long of Pierre, South Dakota, knew the old fighter well. He once arrested him at Rosebud, while serving as United States Deputy Marshal, and they became very friendly. The chief told him he did kill Tom Custer. "I didn't shoot him," he said, "I killed him with a club, because he slapped my face when I was bound and a prisoner at Fort Niobrara." That was the extent of his doing.

Judge Ernest knew many of the Indians who had taken part in the fighting. One of these, Two Bears, he always declared, was the finest gentlemen he had ever known. Asked to tell the story of the battle, Two Bears replied: "The young men came in early in the morning and said the soldiers were coming up the river. The war chiefs told us to get our ponies and rifles. The soldiers were soon seen. There was a great deal of shooting. Then all was still."

Custer was born at New Rumley, Ohio, December 5, 1839, and was still very young when made major-general of cavalry. He was handsome as well as daring, six feet one inch in height, with a long, drooping blond mustache and golden locks that grew down to his shoulders and tossed on the wind as he rode. He wore a uniform made to his own liking—a black-velvet jacket, tight black-velvet trousers that ended in long boots, to which were attached large spurs. He wore his insignia on his sleeve and a broad slouch hat topped his waving hair. His locks had been cut short upon entering the Indian country as being too tempting to Sioux scalp-seekers.

Custer's body was brought east and interred in the Soldier's Rest at West Point. The troopers were buried where they fell, each grave marked with a white stone. It is our smallest and greatest National Cemetery.

With astuteness of the highest order, Sitting Bull and his fellow chiefs kept themselves out of harm's way, working toward the Canadian frontier, having in mind to cross the line into safety when the pursuit became too hot. The defeat of Custer caused a halt in the military proceedings. Terry and Crook retired from the conflict and the task was turned over to Nelson A. Miles. Under his persistent pursuit, the Sioux crossed into Canada and mocked at Uncle Sam. The Canadian Crows made them welcome, though ancient foes, and finally, General Miles had to coax them back on their own terms. Custer was never avenged.

The Indians were established at the Rosebud Agency, where they lived in peace until December 15, 1890, when an attempt by the Indian police to break up a ghost dance led to the last Indian affray

in our annals. Sitting Bull was killed at a point
called Wounded Knee, in the course of the brief
conflict. No harm had resulted from the dance,
but the Indian agent feared the outcome of reviving
old customs which had been forbidden by the
government.

I recall General Miles once saying that he took
no pride in his operations against the Sioux; that
he had never known one who was not a warrior, a
gentleman and a man of honor. Rain-in-the-Face,
he told the writer, was an extraordinary man.
Once when being initiated into a higher order of
Sioux society, he had hung ten hours from the roof
of a medicine lodge suspended by thongs inserted
in the muscles of his chest.

Reno was dismissed from the service for failing
to support Custer in his reckless enterprise.

CHAPTER VIII

GRANT'S ADMINISTRATION

A Period of Corruption and Confusion—The President Well-Meaning and Much Imposed upon—Achievements of Real Value to the Country—Settling the Alabama Dispute—Ending of Inflation—His Reelection—The Tragedy of Horace Greeley.

IT IS fair to the memory of Ulysses S. Grant to say that he did not desire the presidency. Before the war, he had been a Democrat, and was not for or against slavery. He would have much preferred to remain at the head of the army, but, as he reasoned it out, there was a strong chance that any candidate other than himself, who might have been named by the Republicans in 1868, would have met defeat, in which case he would, he believed, have lost his high command. To save to himself the reward that was his due for his great service, he therefore accepted the nomination with Schuyler Colfax, of Indiana, who had been speaker of the House, as nominee for vice-president. Horatio Seymour, of New York, and Frank P. Blair, of Missouri, were the candidates of the Democracy. General Grant was elected by a safe but not a large majority. Indeed, but for the disorganization of the white vote in the South, he would probably have been beaten. Seymour and Blair carried New York, New Jersey and Oregon, while Grant had a scant lead in Ohio, Pennsylvania and Indiana. But he won in twenty-six states, having two hundred fourteen electoral votes, while Seymour was victor in eight, with eighty electoral votes. On the popular vote Grant received 3,015,071 ballots, Seymour 2,709,615. The newly enfranchised negroes in the Southern States were responsible for the Republican lead.

Grant's selection by the Republican party came from no impulse to honor or to reward a great soldier, but to save the party. The leaders saw that Lincoln had beaten General George B. McClellan but 407,342 on the popular vote four years before, with all the claims that the president had upon the suffrages of his countrymen, many army companies voting en masse for him in the field. The border states, under military direction, were persuaded to favor him. General Lew Wallace's manipulation of Maryland is a good example. It would have taken little to cause the North to repudiate the war and all its works. Indeed, Lincoln had great fear that it would. The electoral system, which so often prevents the direct exercise of the popular will, and the army were his salvation. In 1868, the reorganized Republican party was not in a healthy condition. It had installed offensive governments in the South, after having seized the border states, such as Kentucky and Missouri, and manufactured a new Republican commonwealth out of a slice of Old Virginia. Even then it was not certain of success, and with all these advantages, Grant's popular majority in 1868 was less than Lincoln's of 1864. With the Union saved and slavery abolished the party was without an issue, and the idealists were pushed aside for spoilsmen. The Democrats were no better off for issues. They were held to be "copperheads" and "skedaddlers" in the North, and traitors in the South. Partisanship without purpose or patriotism ruled on both sides, and the land was full of hatred.

The coming of Grant into power, March 4, 1869, wrought strange social and political changes. Old army comrades pressed him for office on the ground that they had earned the right to a living from their country. Parvenus sought his easily acquired friendship. He had not led a pleasant life, and knew much more about hardship than luxury. To have the country at his feet made him an easy mark. Essentially honest, sincere and well-meaning, he was often deceived and much imposed upon. Legislatively, Roscoe Conkling, the imperious senator from New York, was his master, and behind Conkling, the beautiful Kate Chase Sprague, daughter of the chief justice, ruled. Whisky kings who enriched themselves by frauds upon the internal revenues, and contractors who cheated by charging for services which they did not perform corrupted public officials. Privilege-seeking lobbyists crowded the capitol. Worse than all, soldiers and party leaders who had saved the country did their best to bedevil the result. Andrew Johnson had, of course, been an outcast, while the attempt to remove him from office left him powerless.

Grant's coming, which should have cleared the skies and set the government in order, did nothing of the sort. Of his two terms in office, it is difficult to determine which was the worse. The fault, however, was not his, but that of his party, and the dishonest greedy element produced by the times.

The major scandals, such as Radical Reconstruction, Black Friday and the Credit Mobilier, have been covered in previous chapters. It remains to deal with the details of other episodes, creditable and discreditable, that marked the period of his rule. He had ill luck at the beginning in forming a Cabinet. For secretary of war, he selected his closest army friend, Major-General John A. Rawlins, an excellent choice. For secretary of the treasury, he chose Alexander T. Stewart, the great New York dry-goods merchant, as a sop to Croesus, people thought. As an importer who dealt with the Treasury Department through the Custom House, he was ineligible, a fact that was not discovered until several days after he had been nominated and confirmed.

Grant asked Congress to amend the Act of September 2, 1789, which barred merchants from the office, but Charles Sumner's objection to such tinkering with a sound law led to the withdrawal of Stewart's name, to his great vexation. George S. Boutwell, of Massachusetts, was next selected and proved a fortunate choice. The navy was saddled with Adolph E. Borie, a Philadelphian enriched by the war, who had fastened himself on Grant socially, and whose appointment met with popular disfavor. The selection of Jacob D. Cox, of Ohio, for secretary of the interior, offset this error, while the appointment of Judge E. Rockwood Hoar as attorney-general, though giving a second Cabinet seat to Massachusetts, met with approval. Making John A. J. Creswell, of Maryland, postmaster-general, proved a blunder. Here again the president's social side misled him. Elihu B. Washburne, of Illinois, named for secretary of state, gave satisfaction. He was one of a remarkable Maine family that furnished three governors to as many states, who had served the country with distinction, and whose influence had made Grant a brigadier in 'sixty-one. His stay in office was short, however, as he soon resigned to become minister to France, where his services during the War of 1870-71 and the trying period of the Commune remain memorable. His place was taken by Hamilton Fish, of New York, son of Nicholas Fish, who had been George Washington's aide-de-camp, and who was connected with the Schuylers and Hamiltons by ties of blood. He was rich and distinguished. His conduct of his high office was unexceptionable.

The first act of the new administration was to push away the greenback cloud. Congress passed a law reaffirming the country's pledge to redeem all currency in coin. The vicious Tenure of Office Act, under which President Johnson had been put on trial, was modified, very largely by the votes of men who had passed it in an effort to dominate Johnson. Grant recommended its total repeal in a message of December 6, 1869. The amended statute held, however, until March 3, 1887, when Senator George Frisbie Hoar caused it to be wiped off the books, President Grover Cleveland approving. The income tax, first imposed in 1861 as a war measure, expired by legal limitation December 31, 1871, which took that offensive and corrupting form of levy off the country's back. It had been reduced to two and one-half per cent.

Reverdy Johnson, of Maryland, had succeeded Charles Francis Adams as minister to England, and managed to annoy America a good deal with effusive "hands-across-the-sea" speeches. There was much feeling against England over the affair of the building and delivery of the *Alabama,* and over other aid given the Confederacy, and a decided tendency to deal harshly with Britain. Johnson had, however, concluded an engagement with Lord Clarendon that subjected all claims between the two countries dating back to July 26,

1853, to arbitration. This was while William H. Seward was secretary of state, January 14, 1869, but the Senate would have none of it, and the treaty continued to lie on the table. The new Senate rejected it, fifty-four to one, after Charles Sumner had assailed the agreement as showing no signs of contrition on the part of the lion.

Here the president showed his high qualities of wisdom and prudence. Secretary Fish took the matter in hand and emerged from the situation with great credit. The Fenians had been raiding Canada, and Sumner had given expression to the thought that the Lady of the Snows should be annexed in compensation for British sins. Sumner was chairman of the Senate Committee on Foreign Affairs, and very powerful. Through his influence, John Lothrop Motley, the distinguished historian of *The Rise of the Dutch Republic,* had replaced Johnson in London. Fish had forestalled an embroilment with Spain by preventing the recognition of the Cuban insurgents, the Ten Years' War being then at its height. He next ran into a shirt-sleeves complication wrought by Grant at the instance of a group of promoters which was an effort to annex Santo Domingo, where these gentlemen had acquired numbers of valuable concessions from President Baez, who, being hard-pressed by rebels, was anxious to sell out. The matter was first set in motion by a plan to rent the Bay of Samana for a naval station. This came through General O. E. Babcock, one of Grant's army friends who had been made his assistant-secretary and the bulk of whose assistance consisted in getting Grant into scrapes. He visited Santo Domingo and brought back a scheme to lease Samana for one hundred fifty thousand dollars a year. This failing to interest the Cabinet, he made another trip to the distressed coffee-colored republic and returned with a treaty of annexation, in which it was provided that the United States was to pay a one million five hundred thousand dollar debt as a reward for taking over Baez and his troubles, Hayti remaining independent. The Cabinet was quite amazed at this offhand act, while Senator Sumner, as chairman of the Senate Committee on Foreign Affairs, would have none of it. To soothe Grant, however, a commission composed of Benjamin F. Wade, Andrew D. White and S. G. Howe, was sent on the *Tennessee,* the navy's biggest warship, to investigate the subject. This body reported elaborately but non-committally on April 5, 1871, Grant sending in their statement and leaving it up to the Senate, which declined to take further action. Grant was deeply vexed at Sumner's attitude. The incident cost the senator his important chairmanship and led to the removal of Motley as minister to England because he was counted Sumner's man. The feud ended only at Sumner's death.

The proposition to trade claims for Canada

continued very much alive, while England, seeing
the possibility of a world conflict in the Franco-
Prussian War, dealt gently with the folly. By the
device of a Joint High Commission, the peril of a
clash was warded off. Secretary Fish, Attorney-
General Hoar, Justice Samuel Nelson, General
Robert C. Schenck, the draw-poker expert, and
Senator George H. Williams, of Oregon, a friend
of Grant, were the American members. Sir
Edward Thornton, the British Minister, Earl De
Grey, Sir Stafford Northcote, Professor Moun-
tague Bernard, of Oxford, and Sir John A.
MacDonald, Premier of Canada, represented
England. The sessions were held in Washington
and ended in a convention establishing an Arbitra-
tion Tribunal of Five, to be appointed by the
United States, England, Brazil, Italy and Switzer-
land, through their ruling heads. This was carried
to a successful conclusion. The Tribunal met at
Geneva and settled the Alabama Claims with an
award of fifteen million dollars, leaving a bright
spot in the record of civilization.

Against this great achievement there must now
be recorded a multitude of mistakes. In the war
on Sumner, Grant wished to rid himself of Attorney-General Hoar. He therefore named him
for the Supreme Bench, but the unruly Senate
rejected the nomination. Grant then asked for his
resignation. It was instantly granted, on June 15,
1870. In the fall, General Cox gave up the port-

GRANT'S ADMINISTRATION

folio of the Interior Department. Grant had tried to force his hand in yielding to a rascally land claim in California, made by one McGarrahan. The honest secretary quit on October third. The crushing of Sumner put the Senate in the hands of Zachariah Chandler, of Michigan, Roscoe Conkling, of New York, and Simon Cameron, of Pennsylvania. Conkling was honest but imperious. The others looked out for number one. Benjamin F. Butler's influence took the place of that of Sumner and Hoar. He led the House of Representatives in a riot of political looting.

Judge Hoar was succeeded in the Cabinet by Amos Tappan Akerman, a New Hampshire man and Dartmouth graduate who had settled at Elberton, Georgia, in 1859, and joined the Confederacy, holding office in the quartermaster's department during the war. He became a Republican and radical reconstructionist, receiving as a reward the appointment of United States district attorney for Georgia. He remained in office a little more than a year, inconspicuously, and resigned in 1872 to make way for Edwards Pierrepont. He was helpful to Georgia in her troubles during the mid-stages of reconstruction.

The District of Columbia under Grant was transformed from a mud-hole into a fine and well-made city. Laid out by Major L'Enfant, a distinguished engineer imported for the purpose during Washington's administration, the plans were mostly on paper, while stray hogs did the road-making. Congress, in 1871, organized the district into a territory for its better government, but really to make a place for A. R. Shepard, a friend of the president. Shepard had much of the character of Tweed, and followed his lavish ways in the matter of public improvements. He paved the streets with asphalt, then a novelty, produced parks in the squares from which the boulevards radiated, and gave the city the form to which it owed its later attractiveness. But, in doing all this, he stole liberally. Congress, in alarm at the cost, abolished the territorial form of government as a means of getting rid of Shepard, in 1874, substituting therefor a capital commission. The president, quite unmoved by a report which told plainly of Shepard's peculations, named him as a member of the commission. The Senate rejected the nomination. Shepard had also taken on Tweed's super-designation of boss. It took some time to break his power, but at last he gave way, with prison in plain sight. A quick departure to Mexico and oblivion saved him from punishment. It is one of the strangest of manifestations that sundry American cities have had to wait for a rogue to make them fit to live in. Quite naturally, Grant's devotion to Shepard did not improve the odor of his administration.

The luxuries of the average American of the day were a good horse, good cigars and good whisky. Grant liked all three and had pined for them in his years of poverty. The presidency gave him what he craved, and he took to all, eagerly. For company, he liked men of the same tastes. Yet he was not low or vulgar. Being a shy man, he was brought out only by a good deal of attention, and this the flamboyant self-seekers provided, supplying along with it a fine line of rapacity and scandal.

Presents poured in on the president, ranging from fast horses to superior whisky and cigars. Even Abdul Hamid, Sultan of Turkey, sent two specimens of fine horse-flesh, Arabian steeds named Linden Tree and Leopard. Benefits also accrued to his own and his wife's relations. Taken together they formed a greedy brood. The general saw no reason why he should reject manifestations of gratitude and esteem, or repel the rewards due his great services to the country. He would have sold nothing, but was willing to give and receive much in innocent gratification of desires. Naturally, scandals followed. One of the earliest was that over "Seneca Stone," a monopoly enjoyed for a flourishing moment by the Maryland Stone Company, an organization got together by H. D. Cooke, Governor of the District of Columbia. He held two hundred forty thousand dollars' worth of the stock. President Grant was credited with owning twenty-five thousand dollars in its certificates, his brother-in-law and secretary, General F.

T. Dent, ten thousand dollars; General O. E. Babcock, another secretary, ten thousand dollars; Major-General Joseph K. Barnes, eleven thousand dollars; Paymaster-General B. W. Brice, fourteen thousand dollars; Commissory-General M. C. Meigs, nine thousand dollars; General Nathan Meichler, Superintendent of Public Buildings and Grounds, ten thousand dollars; and Colonel John W. Forney, Secretary of the Senate, ten thousand dollars. It was not pretended that any of these military gentlemen had paid for their stock, while the stone came in for liberal use in improvements about the capitol, and in the national cemeteries, while some of the stockholders were presumably influential in securing contracts. The Democratic press railed at it, but there was no open action taken against the concern. It made, however, another black mark.

Resentment among the better class of Republicans, those who had joined the party through sympathy with its ideals, and others who had had a share in shaping it, was not long in developing, under such conditions. The movement to purge the party had its start in Missouri, where Carl Schurz had become associated with Doctor Emil Preetorious in the publication of the *Westliche Post*. The German element in St. Louis, mainly exiles of 1848 and their relatives or descendants, strongly supported Schurz, while the adventurers who fastened upon the state controlled the party.

[272]

GRANT'S ADMINISTRATION

As a result, B. Gratz Brown, Schurz and Preetorious, aided by a young and enthusiastic associate-
editor of the *Post,* Joseph Pulitzer, started a
movement that redeemed the state politically and
led to the formation of an independent Republican
party, which gathered a strong following in the
East and Middle West, thanks to the influence of
Samuel Bowles, speaking through the *Springfield
Republican,* and Murat Halstead, thundering at
the gates of corruption in the *Cincinnati Commercial.* In New York, Horace Greeley's *Tribune*
and William Cullen Bryant's *Evening Post* fed
the fires of party revolt. Chicago was lit up by
Joseph Medill and the *Tribune.*

The result was a National Convention, held at
Cincinnati, on May 1, 1872, at which the fatal
mistake was made of nominating Horace Greeley.
The badly led Democrats, instead of welcoming
this party split and maneuvering to take advantage of it, endorsed Greeley and B. Gratz Brown,
his associate on the ticket, at a convention held in
Baltimore on July ninth. The Republicans met
in Philadelphia on the fifth of June and renom-
inated Grant without opposition. Schuyler Colfax
was dropped from the vice-presidency and Senator Henry Wilson, of Massachusetts, named in his
stead. Greeley's change of face roused great
antagonism.

"Mr. Greeley is in bad company," wrote Henry
Ward Beecher, his colleague in former liberalisms.

[273]

"He is in a false position. He is abandoning his old friends and taking council with his enemies. He is on the wrong path."

This expressed a wide sentiment. Greeley had lost much of his old following by going bail for Jefferson Davis. The *Tribune* had become a scold, not an influence. "Copperhead" Democrats could not swallow a man who had so terribly belabored their party. The consequence was that Greeley fell between two stools and was dreadfully defeated. Georgia, Kentucky, Missouri, Tennessee and Texas alone were for him. Grant had two hundred sixty-four electoral votes, and about seven hundred fifty thousand lead on the popular ballot. Worse than this, Greeley's personal fortunes shared in the disaster. He had gone into the campaign leaving the *Tribune* in editorial charge of Whitelaw Reid and John Hay, both young men from Ohio. Hay had been one of Lincoln's secretaries, and Reid, the *Tribune's* war correspondent, earning much odium from great generals by his strictures on their conduct, notably those on Grant and Sherman at Shiloh. The new editors of the *Tribune* handled the paper well so far as editorial labor could effect it, but circulation shrank and business faded.

Greeley was but a small shareholder, and his associates saw in their holdings a poor investment, which made them agreeable to a proposition from William Orton, President of the Western Union

Telegraph Company, to take over the paper, with the plan in mind of putting Schuyler Colfax, now in need of a job, in Greeley's chair. He had secured an option on enough *Tribune* stock to carry out his purpose, when late in the campaign the Credit Mobilier scandal came to light and Colfax became impossible.

Greeley returned from the campaign broken and overstrained to learn that he had lost the *Tribune*. His wife died a week before his defeat, and three weeks after election he left this world from the effects of an attack of brain fever on November 29, 1872. Orton thus had the option on his hands, with no editor and a bigger financial risk than he cared to carry. At this juncture, he turned to Jay Gould, who kindly relieved him of the burden. Mr. Reid, who had expected to find himself out of place, interested William Walter Phelps, and with his backing, acquired the stock from Gould.

There was a widespread popular revulsion at Mr. Greeley's death. He had been so brave, so unselfish, so truly a journalist and friend of liberty, that the land underwent a quick change of attitude, ashamed that it had so belabored him during the campaign, when he had been cartooned and assailed mercilessly. True, he had never given quarter himself, but the people realized that with all his mistakes, and they were not a few, he was a great editor, a great man and a great patriot in the real sense of the word. And he was not old—only sixty-two. A full decade of vigor and usefulness lay before him when he was cut off by the luckless nomination and its cruel consequences. The nation, which had sacrificed him, went into mourning. New York raised a statue to his memory, and he lives as one of America's immortals.

Quite reasonably, Grant felt that he had been roundly endorsed by his countrymen. The Democrats had elected Thomas A. Hendricks governor of Indiana by about one thousand, one hundred majority. All else in the North was Republican of the Grant pattern. There were but nineteen Democrats in the Senate and eighty-eight in the House. A few liberal Republicans squeezed through—five senators and four congressmen. The dominant party had a two-thirds vote in both houses and was seemingly invincible.

On the strength of this, the outgoing Congress voted itself an increase of salary from five thousand dollars to seven thousand five hundred dollars a year, and not content with this, made the act retroactive. The indignation that followed this, was unmeasured. Congressmen and senators alike were arraigned by their constituents. Some were shamed into returning the increment to the Treasury. The storm would not down, with the result that the Forty-third Congress, at its first session, repealed the increase.

The campaign had not been pleasant for Grant,

despite the triumphal end. He had been violently assailed, the independent press being much more ably manned than that of his defenders, while the facts arrayed against him were damning. He felt the sting keenly enough to assert in his inaugural address that he had "been the subject of abuse and slander scarcely ever equalled in political history," and "gratefully accepted" the victory as a vindication. That he was unconscious of doing badly would seem clear enough from the fact that his second administration was no improvement on the first. Discreditable appointments were made, such as that of Thomas C. Murphy for collector of New York and William E. Simmons for collector of Boston. The last was secured for Simmons by Butler and caused a Bay State storm. These appointments and their kind roused Carl Schurz, then in the Senate from Missouri, Lyman Trumbull, Senator from Illinois, and Congressman T. A. Jenckes, of Rhode Island, to father the beginning of what was to become a system of civil service. Grant at first accepted the rules in principle, but neglected them in practise.

May 7, 1873, Chief Justice Salmon Portland Chase died in New York City. He was born in Cornish, New Hampshire, January 14, 1808, and was a nephew of Philander Chase, Bishop of the Episcopal Church and one of the founders of Kenyon College, Ohio, where the younger Chase graduated and so lodged in Ohio. From this state he was elected United States senator in 1849, serving until 1855, when he retired to Ohio, to become governor for four years. Lincoln made him secretary of the treasury. He served during the heavy period of war finance and was appointed chief justice in 1864. This place he filled with great dignity and wisdom. His death left a vacancy calling for unusual care in filling. Grant flouted the opportunity to improve his administrative record by appointing George H. Williams, of Oregon, his attorney-general. Williams was not only incompetent but was believed to be corrupt, the acceptance of a pair of horses and an open carriage from certain self-seeking admirers causing him to be dubbed "Landaulet" Williams.

His appointment raised a great storm, and the Senate refused to accept him. The nomination was withdrawn, only to make way for another mistake. Grant now appointed Caleb Cushing, of Massachusetts, who had presided over the Democratic Convention at Charleston in 1860 where the party split. Cushing had a distinguished public career. Born January 17, 1800, at Salisbury, a town famous in history as the stopping point of Quaker persecution in Massachusetts, he had been a member of Congress, 1835-1843; United States commissioner to China, 1843-44; colonel and brigadier-general in the Mexican War, and attorney-general in Franklin Pierce's administration, 1853-1857. He next played a large part on behalf of the United States as one of the counsel appearing before the Geneva Tribunal, 1871-1872, out of which came the award of fifteen million dollars against Great Britain and the peaceful settlement of the so-called Alabama Claims growing out of the destruction of American shipping by English equipped Confederate cruisers during the Civil War. Grant liked him, and of his ability as a lawyer there could be no question. He was reputed to be more than sharp in his legal practise and in business, but the digging up of a letter written to Jefferson Davis after the formation of the Confederate States, but before Sumter, recommending a man for consideration in the new "Republic," proved his undoing. Davis was secretary of war in Pierce's Cabinet, of which Cushing was a member, and they were friends. For that matter, Davis had many friends in the North, having spent some of his summers in Portland, Maine, where he was very popular.

Quite naturally, in a bloody-shirt period the author of such a note as follows would not do:

Washington, March 20, 1861.

Dear Sir:

Mr. Archibald Roane, for the last six or seven years a clerk in the Attorney-General's office, desires from me a letter of introduction to you, and he desires it not in the view of anticipating administrative favors, but that he may have the honor of your personal intercourse. Of this I take pleasure in assuring you he is eminently worthy. A southern man by birth, family, and affection, he has carefully studied and ably discussed, in Mr. De Bow's *Review* and other southern works, the lamentable events which have been gradually undermining, and have at length overthrown the American Union. Whilst a practical man, he is also a ripe and accomplished scholar with, indeed, predominant literary tastes and habits. In the discharge of his official duties he has combined in a singular degree the purest integrity and most enlightened intelligence, with modest contentment in his lot, having more than once declined offices of more conspicuous employment in the public service. He now resigns his present office from sentiments of devotion to that which alone he can feel to be his country, namely, the Confederate States, from one of which (Texas) he was appointed. I most heartily commend him as a gentleman and a man to your confidence and esteem. And I am, with the highest consideration, your obedient servant.

C. CUSHING.

Hon. Jefferson Davis,
President, The Confederate States.

With great reluctance Grant withdrew Cushing's name. He became minister to Spain until 1877, and died at Newburyport, Massachusetts, January 2, 1879. A busy revenue cutter long bore his name.

President Grant now named Morrison R. Waite, of Ohio, a lawyer of local note who had served with Cushing before the Geneva Tribunal.

He was promptly confirmed and proved to be a happy selection. He was born at Lyme, Connecticut, November 29, 1816, and died at Washington, March 23, 1888, having served fourteen years on the bench with distinction. A Yale graduate and a profound student, he ranks with the best of the men who have presided over the Supreme Court.

The wedding of the president's daughter, Nellie, to Algernon G. F. Sartoris, was made the occasion for great display on May 21, 1874. It was the third to be held in the White House. Sartoris was a young Englishman of twenty-three, grandson of Charles Kemble, the eminent English actor, and a nephew of the famous "Fanny" or Frances Anne Kemble, who had married Pierce Butler, of South Carolina, but who left him after a stay on his plantation that caused her to become bitterly opposed to slavery. Sartoris was her sister Adelaide's son. He had the magnificent Mrs. Siddons for a grand-aunt. Miss Grant was a gentle, well-liked girl. The young couple had met on a trans-Atlantic steamer eighteen months before, with the common fatal result of propinquity. Grant gave his daughter ten thousand dollars and the country showered her with gifts, many of great value. Sartoris was described as amiable, talented and a "good singer of songs." Following the wedding Sartoris and his bride departed at once for Europe. Their union was destined to be unhappy, and in time they separated.

[281]

THE DREADFUL DECADE

June 29, 1874, the Freedman's Savings and Trust Company, with head-offices in Washington, closed its doors. Its affairs had been subjected to legal scrutiny, with the discovery that it was best to wind up the affairs of the institution. Frederick Douglass, the celebrated negro orator, was president, and it represented an effort to inculcate a taste for saving money among the former slaves. The results were disastrous and deplorable. Three "commissioners" were appointed to liquidate the concern, the chief of whom was J. A. J. Creswell, of Maryland, a friend of Grant. He was forced out of the postmaster-generalship just in time to slip into the new position, Marshall Jewell resigning his place as minister to Russia to succeed Creswell in the Postoffice Department. The commission dozed along for years, paying but thirty per cent. back to the victims and collecting $318,753.64 for their own services in so doing.

Coincident with this, the Freedman's Bureau, established in reconstruction days to act as guardian for the unchained bondmen, came in for a caustic overhauling, which included the course of its head, Major-General Oliver Otis Howard, the "Christian Soldier." While he was whitewashed by the majority of a board of fellow army officers, the case as reviewed by Judge Advocate-General Holt, at Grant's instance, proved Howard unfit for the trust. He was therefore sent back into active service as Commander of the Department of the Columbia, on July third, to refresh his fame by hunting down Chief Joseph of the Nez Perces, after a stern chase of something like eighteen hundred miles.

The heavy impost placed upon distilled spirits in an effort to provide revenue for the national government gave great opportunities for frauds, which were practised in all the centers of whisky-making—Louisville, Cincinnati, Peoria and most of all in St. Louis, where a corrupt ring was formed that had its agent in the White House. The resulting scandal, therefore, came closer to the president than any one of the numerous others that developed during his term of office.

Grant, while a resident in St. Louis after his retirement from the regular army, had made a number of friends to whom he was under obligations, and when he came into power he rewarded them with office, exciting a hostility among the better class of Republicans that became an initial factor in the revolt of 1872. Their open opposition caused Grant to feel much uneasiness for the future, desiring as he did a second term. Following his usual habit, he stood more firmly by his friends, who took this as an encouragement to go to any length in "saving" the party and incidentally filling their own pockets. To this end Brevet Brigadier-General John McDonald, an illiterate but energetic man who had served with Grant in his Vicksburg campaign, was appointed supervisor of Internal Revenue for the district which included St. Louis. He had set himself up as a collector of claims against the government, but a fire destroying much of his evidence, he was induced to take the three-thousand-dollar job to help Grant against his foes. One of these was William McKee, publisher of the *Democrat,* of which William Grosvenor was editor. McKee was taken into the ring and the paper reversed its policy. Grosvenor declined to be a party to the shift, and resigned.

Meanwhile, through McDonald, the ring hitched up with General O. E. Babcock, President Grant's secretary, who received in cash, according to McDonald, thirty thousand dollars besides numerous costly presents. The excuse behind McDonald's action was that the money was needed to keep the party alive and secure Grant's retention in office. This accomplished, however, the operations did not cease. They were needed now, according to McDonald, to secure a third term for the president. He professed to believe that Grant, through Babcock, was fully cognizant of what was going on. During a visit to St. Louis and to his farm at Galena, Grant received from McDonald a fine pair of horses, with side-bar buggy and gold-mounted harness, for which he gave three dollars in return for a receipt for one thousand seven hundred dollars, representing the value of the outfit.

Thus matters went on swimmingly until Benjamin H. Bristow, of Kentucky, became secretary of the treasury. He was honest, did not like Grant or his following, and had ambitions to become president. From George W. Fishback, publisher of the *St. Louis Globe,* a rival of McKee, he learned of the existence of the St. Louis ring and began an investigation that revealed the truth, which was that the revenue from the great American tonic produced in McDonald's territory was paying about half what was due from it in the way of internal revenue. He took office in June, 1874. The Fishback information came to him in February, 1875, and by May tenth he had established his case, involving General Babcock and a full line of Grant's St. Louis friends. Thirty-two raids were made.

Indictments were found and former Senator John B. Henderson was engaged as special counsel, after ·McDonald and Babcock had made great efforts to head off action.

W. D. W. Barnard, a St. Louis banker, close up to the worried crowd, wrote Grant a letter in July, 1875, while he was summering at Long Branch, in which he charged that Henderson was an enemy and was prosecuting men whose only crime was backing the administration. This note Grant sent to Bristow on July twenty-ninth, with this historic endorsement:

Let no guilty man escape if it can be avoided.

Be especially vigilant, or instruct those engaged in the prosecution of the fraud to be against all who intimate that they have high influence to protect—or to protect them. No personal consideration should stand in the way of performing public duty.

Buford Wilson, Solicitor for the Treasury, believed Babcock guilty and probably thought Grant possessed guilty knowledge. He pressed hard on Babcock's trail, to the deep anger of the president who considered the real animus of the prosecution to be against himself. He interfered visibly to protect his friend, despite the ringing letter to Bristow. The United States Commissioner, one Douglass, was among those hampered in his work. This exasperated Henderson, who in the course of the trial of William O. Avery remarked:

"What right had Babcock to go to Douglass to induce him to withdraw his agents? Douglass was placed in his position to see that the revenue laws of the government were properly enforced. What business, then, had Douglass with him? When an official goes into office, he should be free and independent of all influence except that of law, and if he recognizes any other master, then this government is tumbling down. What right had the president to interfere with Commissioner Douglass in the proper discharge of his duties, or with the secretary of the treasury? None, and Douglass showed a lamentable weakness of character when he listened to Babcock's dictates. He should either have insisted that his orders, as they existed, be carried out, or should have resigned his office. Now, why did Douglass bend the supple hinges of his knee and permit any interference by the president? This was Douglass' own business, and he stood responsible for it under his official oath. He was bound to listen to no dictation from the president, Babcock, or any other officer, and it was his duty to see that that order was carried out or resign. Would that we had officials who possessed more of that sterner stuff of which the office holders of olden times were made! Why do they not leave their office when they can not remain there honorably? Is it to be that because a man holds an office at the hands of another, he is to be a bonded slave?"

W. D. W. Barnard heard this, and wired the words to Grant. As a result, Henderson was displaced as counsel, a proceeding that naturally confirmed the worst suspicions of Grant. McDonald and Colonel John A. Joyce, his assistant, were convicted and sent to the Jefferson City penitentiary. Babcock was tried, but found "not guilty," on February 24, 1876. He returned to take his place in the White House. Grant went into his office and for two long hours the two sat behind the closed door. When Grant came out, his face was set and worn. Babcock at once departed and did not return. He was not turned out upon a cold world, however, but received the appointment of superintendent of public buildings. There is no doubt whatever that he was guilty of conniving at the frauds. How much did Grant know? The question must remain unanswered.

McDonald, who had kept silent under prosecution and imprisonment, became tired of jail and sent his counsel to Grant with a letter demanding pardon on threat of exposure. He was pardoned. He next sought the release of Joyce. This was promised, but not given. President Hayes, however, set him free. He was a strange, flamboyant character, who, among other distinctions, claimed to have written *Laugh and the World Laughs with You,* a lyric that came from the pen of Ella Wheeler Wilcox.

The whisky-ring scandal and the cry of Cæsarism, raised mainly by Whitelaw Reid in the *New York Tribune,* killed any chance for the desired third term. In 1880, when Roscoe Conkling with three hundred and six unflinching votes sought to rename Grant in the National Republican Convention, McDonald published a book purporting to tell the whole story. Joyce probably wrote it. He there claims that Grant knew all that was going on, that William McKee received three hundred thousand dollars, which enabled him to buy the *St. Louis Globe* and consolidate it with the *Democrat.* He, too, had been sentenced to two years in jail, and to pay a fine of ten thousand dollars. In six months Grant remitted the fine and the rest of the sentence. The illicit profits of the ring were estimated at something like two million, five hundred thousand dollars.

Out of the friction, Bristow and Marshall Jewell, Postmaster-General, threw up their jobs. The administration was wrecked and Grant's name had become anathema in the land.

John A. Rawlins died September 9, 1869, after a few brief months of service, and in filling his place Grant made one of his alternating mistakes in appointing William W. Belknap secretary of war on October thirteenth. He was a native of Newburgh, New York, who had served with Grant at Shiloh and Vicksburg, with Sherman in the Atlanta campaign and hailed from Iowa at the time of his elevation to the Cabinet. He had been brevetted a major-general and was internal revenue collector for the state, when selected. His wife was a showy woman who fell readily into the easy ways of meeting the high cost of living during the Grant era at Washington. Following the whisky-ring scandal, another broke, seriously involving the secretary of war. The Committee on Military Expenditures in the War Department, headed by Hiester Clymer, of Pennsylvania, came upon serious evidences of corruption in Belknap's domain. Post-traderships were valuable in those days, and it was brought out that the secretary was sharing in the profits of at least one of these fat opportunities, by operating through George P. Marsh, a friend of his late wife. She appears to have made the arrangement with Marsh, by which John S. Evans, who held the privilege at Fort Sill, in the Indian Territory, gave up twelve thousand dollars a year to Marsh, who divided with Mrs. Belknap, and, after her death, with the secretary himself. The twelve thousand dollars was in time reduced to six thousand dollars a year and shared as before. In all the Belknaps had taken forty thousand dollars from the trader.

When the report was made on March 2, 1876, Belknap at once resigned. Grant accepted his departure with "regret," and would no doubt have stood by him, as he did Babcock. Belknap was impeached, despite his abandonment of office, and placed on trial before the Senate. August 1, 1876, that body voted, but failed to convict, the necessary two-thirds being lacking. The vote stood thirty-seven to twenty-five. This does not mean that the twenty-five believed him innocent. All but two thought the Senate had no jurisdiction in view of Belknap's withdrawal from office. The affair added one more broad black mark to the record of Grant's administration at a moment when it could do the most harm—in the midst of a presidential campaign. Belknap dropped out of sight and died at Washington October 13, 1890, on the anniversary of his unfortunate appointment.

GRANT'S ADMINISTRATION

No sadder story remains to be told of Grant's era than the fate of the navy. The president's friend, Borie, was careless and incompetent, if not corrupt. He gave way, after a few months in office, to George M. Robeson, of New Jersey, who survived until the end of the administration. The old ships that had done such stout service during the Civil War were patched up at extravagant rates by favored contractors, while the navy yards became camping grounds for political loafers and centers of corruption. It was hardly safe to send a ship to sea in Robeson's day. While France, England and Italy profited by the lessons of the conflict, we ignored them. Favoritism ruled, and the service, of which the country had always been proud, became a reproach.

CHAPTER IX

TILDEN AND HAYES

Political Conditions in 1876—Rise of a Great Reformer—The Presidential Election a Deadlock—Civil Strife Threatened—The Electoral Commission Keeps Republicans in Power—Mr. Tilden's Sacrifice—Hayes Rights the Ship of State.

THE capture by the Democrats of the House of Representatives in 1874 led to high hopes in the party of securing the presidency in 1876. Despite the disturbed state of the South, which interfered with its solidity, the North had turned upon the Republican party. The scandals of the Grant administration, the greed of the "soldier" element, and the general absence of patriotism and common honesty in the party management, had caused many independents to stay out of the fold after the Greeley fiasco. There had come into the scheme of affairs, a very able Democrat, Samuel Jones Tilden. Such justice as had been handed the Tweed ringsters was due to his acumen. As a railroad lawyer he had done much to straighten out the curves in financing the enterprises, intervening between promoters and investors. He was past sixty when he consented to go to the legislature of New York, and his next step was to become governor, following Alonzo B. Cornell, who had succeeded Hoffman, and to restore Democratic rule at Albany. As governor he cleaned out the rings that infested the capital, notably one fathered by James J. Belden, of Syracuse, that fattened on the state's canal system, which had been a most profitable investment for the commonwealth and a tempting field for political exploitation. This won him great acclaim and, considering the substantial majority behind him, made his selection as the Democratic nominee for the presidency inevitable. Besides this he was rich, a consideration of importance in an American campaign before the system of "frying" fat corporations came into vogue. Mr. Tilden was duly nominated at the convention which met at St. Louis, June twenty-eighth, with Thomas A. Hendricks as his running-mate. Both were conservatives of the most concrete sort.

The election of Samuel J. Randall, of Pennsylvania, to succeed Michael C. Kerr, of Indiana, as speaker of the House, after the death of the latter, was a serious political mistake on the part of the Democratic majority. The party was for a low tariff—for as close an approach to free trade as the requirements of revenue would permit. Randall was a Pennsylvania protectionist and belied the principles of the Democratic party. He did the party much mischief, and although a man of honesty and great ability, he unquestionably retarded progress. Randall gave an insincerity to Democratic purposes that seriously handicapped his party's fortunes. In spite of this, it made itself potent through Congress, and with the full restoration of southern rights became and remained the ruling political power in the South.

Thus the negrophile policy of the Republicans, which was political and not philanthropic or based upon a special desire to protect human rights, perpetuated political petrifaction and did nothing but harm to the freedmen. No Republican president, from Grant to the valorous Roosevelt, or from Taft to Coolidge, has ever had the courage to enforce the Thirteenth, Fourteenth or Fifteenth Amendments. They remain monuments of political futility and injustice, vindicating Senator Stewart's theory, however, that they would serve to save the black vote to the Republican party in the North. Their only other effect has been to mar seriously the sacredness of the Constitution.

James G. Blaine, of Maine, stood in the lead for the Republican nomination, bitterly opposed by Roscoe Conkling, of New York, who was himself a candidate after the fading out of third-term hopes for Grant.

The Republican Convention was called to meet at Cincinnati on Wednesday, June 14, 1876, but Mr. Blaine's directing spirit was stilled the Sunday before, June eleventh, by an attack of illness that came upon him in his pew in Doctor Rankin's church on Tenth Street, Washington. The day was intensely hot, and he had walked half a mile to

SAMUEL J. TILDEN

the service. The first report was that he had suffered a shock of paralysis; the official diagnosis
was sunstroke. The real reason was, no doubt, the
terrible strain of the Mulligan inquiry, and the effect of the exposures upon a brain filled with vast
ambition. Scandal and illness came together to
spoil his chances for the presidency.

Despite these odds, his friends rallied strongly.
He led all candidates on the first ballot with two
hundred and eighty-six votes, rising to two hundred and ninety-seven on the second. Conkling
received but ninety-nine, with all his pushing for
the place. Independent Republicanism was in the
saddle to stay. Conkling's vote went off as the
balloting went on. Oliver P. Morton headed him
at the start with one hundred and twenty-four
votes. Rutherford B. Hayes, of Ohio, had the
forty-four votes of his state and seventeen more at
the start, sixty-one in all. By the seventeenth ballot, Hayes had risen to three hundred and eighty-
four, a majority of the seven hundred and fifty-six
delegates, while Blaine had three hundred and
fifty-one. The remaining twenty-one stood for
Benjamin H. Bristow, of Kentucky.

For vice-president, William A. Wheeler, a
congressman from Malone, Franklin County,
New York, tailed the ticket.

Mr. Hayes was a modest man of Vermont descent, who had served bravely in the Civil War,
attaining the rank of brigadier-general, and was,

when nominated, filling his third term as governor of Ohio.

Neither of the candidates was an orator. The campaign was fought mainly by newspapers and Mr. Tilden's pocketbook, which responded liberally to the strain. Hayes was puritanical and a teetotaler. Mr. Tilden possessed the best wine cellar in America, though not a deep drinker of the choice vintages collected. He preferred bouquet to bumpers.

Bayonets still guarded polling places in the South, and carpetbaggers or renegades in the southern service were in power. The true battleground, therefore, appeared to be in the North. Mr. Tilden did not neglect the South. It had been better if he had. The activities of his agents in Florida were to become, in a measure, his undoing. Hayes was the younger man, being fifty-four. He stood for civil service reform and the resumption of specie payments. Tilden was evasive in his letter of acceptance and nearly slipped off the party platform.

The Republicans turned the South into an issue. With Tilden in power it would be again in the saddle, and the struggle of 1861-65 be made vain. Ku Klux performances and local race riots were used to feed the fury and to dye anew the bloody shirt. The presence of many ex-Confederates in Congress was used to support the theory of the come-back of the Confederacy if Tilden won.

Orators of the highest caliber, James G. Blaine,
Oliver P. Morton, Robert G. Ingersoll, George F.
Edmunds, William P. Frye and a host of others
raised the battle-cry. Tilden had no war record;
Hayes had, including a bullet obtained at South
Mountain. Hendricks had been little better than
a "copperhead." Senator Zachariah Chandler, of
Michigan, served as chairman of the Republican
National Committee and Congressman Abram S.
Hewitt, of New York, son-in-lw of Peter Cooper,
the New York philanthropist, headed the Democratic body. Incidentally, Peter Cooper ran for
president on a greenback ticket. He was a mil-
lionaire who had made a fortune out of glue. He
knew how to stick!

Mr. Tilden's "barrel" was much used against
him, though Chandler, the richer of the two, was
gathering funds with a hard hand. One of the
fool charges was that if the Democrats got into
power they would pay for the emancipated slaves
and southern claims for war-damaged property.
As the government was never known to pay anything in the way of claims, this seemed comic, but
was taken seriously enough to draw from Mr.
Tilden a declaration that he would veto any such
measure. The campaign was fought in the one-
hundredth year of national independence and was
destined to produce the most serious test outside of
the Civil War of the stability of the republic.
Frightened at the prospect of losing all they had

gained, the Republicans campaigned with unseemly bitterness. The effect was to arouse vast ill-feeling all over the country. Democrats were persecuted in regions of Republican majorities; political independence brought rough reprisal. Issues that were truly those of government were swept aside and went undiscussed. Partisanship, not public interest, prevailed.

Yet behind all this, the independent element saw the need of checking the rule-or-ruin policies that were being advocated. The Democratic House, under Speaker Michael C. Kerr, had done well, on the whole. Tilden had shown his courage and skill in New York affairs. The shift was distinctly toward him in the North. The Democratic problem was in the South. One of the ugliest items in the excitement was the so-called Hamburg riot of July 8, 1876. A negro militia company paraded on July fourth in Hamburg, South Carolina. Two young men, Thomas J. Butler and Henry Gerzen, his brother-in-law, driving into town, were stopped by Captain Adams of the company, as interrupting the parade. This was resented, and Adams was summoned before Prince Rivers, who was both trial justice and general of militia. General M. C. Butler, afterward United States senator, appeared for the young men. Adams demanded a military trial, and this being refused, declined to appear. White feeling rose, and forty of the black soldiers rallied in their armory under arms. They were asked to give them up, together with their captain, and refused. General Butler claimed that they began firing out of the windows, killing McKee Meriweather, a young white man, at which the whites brought up a cannon and bombarded the blacks. Six of them were killed and three wounded. Fifteen, with their captain, took to the woods. The others were captured. Coming in a presidential campaign, the incident was well used by the Republican orators.

"Tilden Triumphant," was the exultant headline used by the *New York World* on the morning after election, November eighth. "The South calmly puts aside the Rule of its Carpetbaggers," was the continuing comment. The next day the contest was close, the paper claiming one hundred and eighty-eight votes for Tilden, and quoting Hayes as admitting his defeat. Forty-eight votes were placed in the doubtful column. Tilden seemed safe. On the tenth, the *World* claimed two hundred and eight electors for the sage of Gramercy Park and put Florida certainly in his column, though but half its counties were heard from.

Meanwhile, it occurred to the astute mind of John C. Reid, managing editor of the *New York Times,* an expert in political figures, that if Florida could be taken away from Tilden, Hayes would win. He called the attention of Chairman Chandler to the chance, who at once put out a lusty claim. As a starter, President Grant sent orders to General Sherman, Commander of the Army, to instruct General C. C. Augur in Louisiana and General Ruger in Florida "to be vigilant with the forces at their command to preserve peace and good order, and see that the proper and legal boards of canvassers are unmolested in the performances of their duties." To this he added: "Should there be any grounds of suspicion of fraudulent count on either side, it should be reported and denounced at once. No man worthy of the office of president should be willing to hold it if counted in or placed there by fraud."

This dispatch he supplemented with another on the same day to Sherman, sending both from Philadelphia, where he was sojourning. The message to General Sherman read: "Send all troops to Augur he may deem necessary to insure entire and peaceable count of the ballots actually cast. They may be taken from South Carolina unless there is reason to expect outbreak there. The presence of citizens from other states, I understand, is requested in Louisiana, to see that the Board of Canvassers makes a fair count of the vote actually cast. It is to be hoped that representatives and fair men from both parties will go."

This was coincident with the Republican claim that Florida had been carried by two thousand five hundred majority. Troops were at once set in motion. The returning boards in the Southern States soon began to operate. That of South Carolina gave the state to Hayes on the eighteenth of November. Grant's suggestion was followed as to Louisiana and groups of leading men from both parties went South, including John Sherman, Stanley Matthews and James A. Garfield, Republicans; John M. Palmer, Lyman Trumbull and Samuel J. Randall, Democrats. The others were all men of standing. Under Grant's order, troops took possession of the state-house at Columbia and "sustained" Governor D. H. Chamberlain against Wade Hampton, establishing a returning board of bayonets. In Florida, Governor M. L. Stearns, a carpetbagger from Lovell, Maine, was sustained, in the same way, against G. F. Drew, while Governor-elect F. T. Nichols was shut out of the Capitol at Baton Rouge, Louisiana. Vote-counting went on under guard of federal bayonets. Louisiana was practically in a state of civil war, and the other two states were on the edge.

When the electors met in the several states on December sixth and cast their votes, two states remained in dispute and sent conflicting sets of votes—Florida and Louisiana. Oregon also provided a duplication of one vote. A Republican postmaster had been chosen elector who was ineligible under the law, so the Democratic governor refused him a certificate. He resigned both as postmaster and elector and his two colleagues reelected him, while the Republican secretary of state issued a certificate that fixed the three for Hayes. His Democratic opponent organized an electoral board of his own and forwarded two votes for Hayes and one for Tilden to Washington. Hayes had carried the state. The question was purely technical. With Florida and Louisiana, the case was different. Here the states voted for Tilden, and carpetbag returning boards certified electors for Hayes.

Congress could have validated the one vote in Oregon and so have given Tilden the one hundred and eighty-five he needed to secure the election, but the control of the states in the South was considered a large stake, and so, missing this perfectly legal opportunity, the Democrats preferred to go behind the returns in Florida and Louisiana to secure their governors. Curious theories were invoked. Some of the Republicans wished to set Hayes aside and elect Roscoe Conkling. The proposition was made, but the proud "Turkey Cock," as Blaine called him, refused to encourage it. He wanted no office that did not come to him in regular order.

Mr. Tilden wrote a very able brief, entitled: *Who Counts the Electoral Vote?* saying in his prelude:

"The provisions of the Constitution furnish a pretext for some diversity of opinion upon this

[302]

subject, especially when it is investigated under the glamour of fervid partisanship, and when the choice of candidates may depend upon the interpretation those provisions receive. The Constitution provides that the certificates of the votes given by the electors, which are transmitted to the seat of government, shall be delivered to the president of the Senate, and that the president of the Senate shall, in 'the presence of the two Houses of Congress, open all the certificates, and that' they shall then be counted."

But who shall do the counting is not stated, and this Mr. Tilden strove to clarify by reciting the practise of the government as the best guide, and from this he deduced the conclusion that the duty lay with Congress. John Sherman held that the vice-president alone had the power to determine the valid votes. Henry Wilson had died, and Senator T. W. Ferry, of Michigan, sat in his seat as president of the Senate. He was a partisan Republican. Both parties became inconsistent. The Republicans were strong for States Rights, the Democrats for national interference.

There was a Republican majority of seventeen in the Senate and a Democratic lead of seventy-four in the House. By following Mr. Tilden's theory, both houses would have to act. This would have meant no choice, which, in turn, would have thrown the election into the House and to Mr. Tilden. The Republicans held that the Democratic majorities in the South had been obtained by driving negroes from the polls. The Democrats called the Hayes electors fraudulent and insisted on going behind the returns in Florida and Louisiana. Feeling ran high. There were real fears of another civil war. Colonel Henry Watterson announced his purpose to lead a Kentucky army of one hundred thousand on to Washington. This he toned down to mean mere euphony in after years. But the wrath was real, and the chances for a clash considerable. In this stage of the crisis Mr. Tilden was put at a disadvantage by the revelation in the *New York Tribune* of efforts on the part of his nephew, W. T. Pelton, to bribe returning boards in Florida and South Carolina. Tilden was personally blameless in the matter, but it made a smell. Beyond his brief he did nothing, though his popular majority was two hundred and sixty-four thousand.

There was a genuine desire on both sides to avoid civil conflict, and as a result a joint committee of Senate and House was appointed to draw up remedial legislation, which included on the part of the Senate, George F. Edmunds, of Vermont, Oliver P. Morton, of Indiana, F. T. Frelinghuysen, of New Jersey, Roscoe Conkling, of New York, Republicans; Allen G. Thurman, of Ohio, Thomas F. Bayard, of Delaware, M. W. Ransom, of North Carolina, Democrats. The House named Henry B. Payne, of Ohio, Eppa Hunton, of Virginia, Abram S. Hewitt, of New York, William M.

Springer, of Illinois, Democrats; George W. Mc-
Crary, of Iowa, George F. Hoar, of Massachusetts, and George Willard, of Michigan, Republicans. This committee framed a bill, which was
introduced by Senator Edmunds on January
twentieth, with the approval of all his associates
except Oliver P. Morton, which provided for an
electoral commission made up of five senators,
five congressmen and five associate justices of
the Supreme Court. It was passed and became a
law on January twenty-ninth. The Senate selected
George F. Edmunds, Oliver P. Morton, F. T.
Frelinghuysen, Republicans; Allen G. Thurman
and Thomas F. Bayard, Democrats. The House
named Henry B. Payne, Eppa Hunton and
Josiah G. Abbott, of Massachusetts, Democrats;
George F. Hoar and James A. Garfield, Republicans.

The five justices were to be selected by the
associate justices of the Supreme Court assigned
to the First, Third, Eighth and Ninth Circuits,
who should do so in such manner as a majority
might decide. The majority picked Justices
Nathan Clifford, Stephen J. Field, Samuel F.
Miller and William Strong, leaving to them the
choice of the fifth. Clifford, Field and Strong
favored David Davis, of Illinois, but Davis who
had been elected to the Senate, though still on the
bench, deemed himself ineligible and declined.
They then named Joseph P. Bradley.

[305]

THE DREADFUL DECADE

Sessions began on February first, when the two houses met in joint session, and being unable to agree, sent the disputed votes to the commission. The sessions continued all the month, and until five o'clock on the morning of March second, when the presidency was formally awarded to Hayes, as having received one hundred and eighty-five electoral votes to one hundred and eighty-four cast for Mr. Tilden, the commission voting eight to seven on the vitalities. Critical consideration carries the conviction that neither side honestly won the election. Had there been a legal way out both Hayes and Tilden should have been disqualified.

There was great relief at the outcome. Civil strife had been avoided. If the Democrats lost the presidency, they gained tranquillity in the South, the expulsion of the carpetbag governments and the restoration of order and cessation of political warfare. Democratic governors took their seats and the riffraff of adventurers vanished like an ugly dream. Grant, who had grimly prepared to meet any emergency, retired from office, to the general benefit, and departed on a trip around the world. The evil brood he had brought to the capital also went their way. The Republicans were made weaker and the Democrats stronger by the outcome. The *New York Sun* alone was irreconcilable and pictured Hayes with "Fraud" stamped on his brow.

[306]

Bradley was much abused. With the others, he had sworn to act fairly and without partisanship. The others did not obey their oath. On the face of it, neither did he. But he believed he had decided honestly, and on the evidence. The Democrats had taken a risk and lost. That was all there was to it. Mr. Tilden abandoned his leadership in a desire not to bring on another civil war, and deserved credit, which was but grudgingly given him. He could have been nominated and possibly elected in 1880, but declined to venture.

Founded upon a conglomerate cornerstone of anti-slavery, free soil and know-nothingism, in protest against the pro-slavery and conservative policies of the Whigs and Democrats, the Republican party now underwent a singular shift of form. For the two decades of its existence as a national body, it had borne the banner of radicalism. Through all the comment of the period it is termed the party of the radicals. Greeley had made most of it with his fiery pen. Sumner, cold and aristocratic in person, had a furious soul. Slavery was, of course, the bane they wished abolished. This done, the elevation of the negro to the status of a full-fledged citizen became the issue. Politics did this, not popular desire. The evils that grew out of the effort kept the Republicans radical until Hayes was seated.

They then, almost over night, became the party of property. For this, the great campaign fund raised to offset Mr. Tilden's barrel, which only trickled in comparison, was responsible. Zach Chandler began what became the party custom, selling tariff privileges in return for funds used to "bring out the vote," as the excuse is called. Radicalism went without a party, wandering in the wilderness in gypsy groups of Greenbackers and Populists, until it captured the Democratic Convention at Chicago in 1896, Protection paying more and more in each national contest to preserve its privileges. The Republican party faced the danger of recapture by progressives in 1912. This is its peril. Parties do not make issues, issues make parties. They go about like swarms of bees that have left overcrowded hives to seek lodgment where there is room. No party can deem itself safe against unrest; no prophet can tell which one is likely to be seized by vagrant opinion. Leaders are pushed more often than they lead.

Despite the taint upon its title, the Hayes administration was that rare thing in American party history, a success. The president had no political debts to pay, no enemies to avenge himself upon, no friends to reward. He became an executive and nothing else, as the Constitution intended he should be. Conscious of the evils that came from the spoils system, he gave heed to the demand for civil service reform, and, imperfectly supported by legislation, gave it life. While there is a just doubt as to the policy of establishing a permanent force of government employees able to organize in their own interest against that of the public, and protected in their positions by law, it has done away with the evil of office-seeking, with its waste of time and disappointments. It has, however, diminished popular interest in politics and brought a steady decrease in voting. It is difficult to make Americans play a game "with nothing in it."

This diminution of interest has affected all classes. Brigadier-General Lord William Thompson, Air Minister in the British Labor Cabinet, said to me, shortly after its fall in 1925, while on a visit to this country: "I can't find any politics over here. In Great Britain we have nothing but politics."

I replied that in America an election was a sporting event—when the bets were paid, the excitement was over.

"Yes," he said, "I can understand that. But you never get anything done. Why, compared with your average public man, the most conservative British Tory is an anarchist."

The shadow of Prohibition crept over the White House for the first time during the Hayes era. Mrs. Lucy Webb Hayes, the president's wife, was a W. C. T. U. Wine vanished from even state dinners, causing William M. Evarts, the secretary of state and chief-adviser, to say that "water flowed like champagne" at these festivities. There was a Prohibition party long led by

John P. St. John, which had about two hundred and fifty thousand votes and was considered a joke. Men voted the ticket sometimes, in resentment of their own party's policies or candidates. The watery waste added to the unpopularity of the president, and he was unpopular from the start. The Grant element, torn from the flesh-pots, was sore, the spoils-hunters disgruntled, and the privilege-seekers out in the cold. These elements made up the major portions of those concerned with politics.

The people, however, began to find their feet for the first time since 1860. They had wandered in the wilderness for seventeen years and had at last found time and place to sit down. The greenback came within half a cent of par and gambling in gold was no longer an industry or a menace. The grasshoppers lost their appetites for prairie crops. Cattle replaced the buffalo on the great plains. The wheels of industry began to move—slowly—but they turned. Employment began to increase. Without booming or false hopes the country slowly emerged from its demoralized economic conditions and mental disorders.

The South began to look toward the light. It was once more in control of its own affairs. The president took the troops from the capitals and sent them out to hunt Indians. The army was reduced to twenty-five thousand men. The rotten navy was patched up economically and ceased to

Rutherford B. Hayes

be a disgrace. There were no scandals. All at once the country became delightfully dull.

Congress was Democratic, with Samuel J. Randall, a Pennsylvania protectionist, ruling it as speaker. It did no harm. Conkling could rule the Republican Senate, but not Hayes. The "checks and balances" were all in operation. The country for the first time in nearly two decades had a rest from war and turmoil. Even the hand of Fate became still. Great disasters ceased. The steadying influence of sound money upon credit helped the business man and gave the worker bread. Immigrants began to flow in, filling with their energy and ambition the gaps left by war.

Mr. Hayes picked a Cabinet that was in refreshing contrast to that of his predecessor. William M. Evarts, of New York, became secretary of state, John Sherman, of Ohio, secretary of the treasury, George W. McCrary, of Iowa, secretary of war, Richard W. Thompson, of Indiana, secretary of the navy, Charles Devens, of Massachusetts, attorney-general, David M. Key, of Tennessee, postmaster-general, and Carl Schurz, of Missouri, secretary of the interior. The appointments stunned the stalwart Republicans, who had worked their will with Grant. Schurz had been leader of the independent revolt in 1872 and voted for Horace Greeley. Evarts, Key and Devens were accused of the same misdemeanor. Thompson was called too old, and Oliver P. Mor-

THE DREADFUL DECADE

ton's man, though Morton had not backed him. Wailing and gnashing of teeth resounded throughout the land, but the Cabinet held together and was in all respects creditable and efficient. Roscoe Conkling and James G. Blaine were wholly disregarded in making these selections, and upon these two had fallen the divided party leadership. Neither liked the other, but both hated Hayes. The first echo was the resignation of Simon Cameron from the Senate, where he ostensibly represented Pennsylvania, but really himself. His going was interpreted as a protest, but he had arranged to have the vacancy filled by his son, J. Donald Cameron, who notably preserved the family traditions. So the sacrifice was more apparent than real.

The crowning event of the Hayes administration was the resumption of specie payments, agreeable to the Act of 1874. Greenbackism rose in protest against it. Efforts were made in Congress to repeal this article of good faith and honesty. The president was unyielding as Grant had been. So on January 1, 1879, the word of the United States put solid gold behind every dollar in circulation.

The Dreadful Decade had ended.

THE END